TRUE CRIME

ISBN: 9798712391066

Murderers In

New Jersey

The Horrific True Stories of the Garden State Killers

Murderers Everywhere Volume 4

Ryan Becker, Brenda Brown, and True Crime Seven

Table of Contents

Explore the Stories of

The Murderous Minds

A Note

From True Crime Seven

Hi there!

Thank you so much for picking up our book! Before you continue your exploration into the dark world of killers, we wanted to take a quick moment to explain the purpose of our books.

Our goal is to simply explore and tell the stories of various killers in the world: from unknown murderers to infamous serial killers. Our books are designed to be short and inclusive; we want to tell a good scary true story that anyone can enjoy regardless of their reading level.

That is why you won't see too many fancy words or complicated sentence structures in our books. Also, to prevent typical cut and dry style of true crime books, we try to keep the narrative easy to follow while incorporating fiction style storytelling. As to information, we often find ourselves with too little or too much. So, in terms of research material and content, we always try to include what further helps the story of the killer.

Lastly, we want to acknowledge that, much like history, true crime is a subject that can often be interpreted differently. Depending on the topic and your upbringing, you might agree or disagree with how we present a story. We understand disagreements are inevitable. That is why we added this note so hopefully it can help you better understand our position and goal.

Now without further ado, let the exploration to the dark begin!

Introduction

NEW JERSEY, KNOWN AS THE "GARDEN STATE," grows many weeds among the flowers it purports to have. The regions along the shores look like summer playgrounds that coax the salty air ashore. Yet, behind the blowing dunes fall the shadows.

A sandy yard belonging to Richard Biegenwald in Asbury Park—once dug up by the police of the state—yielded no seashells. It did reveal bones and the decomposed remains of innocent girls who never should have died. Some of his grisly internments unearthed the musty brown and brittle bones of little girls he had mutilated.

Among the luxurious Victorian homes of Westfield, there was one house locals called the "Monster House," where an artificially religious man named John List dispatched his family to their heavenly reward. There would be no earthly future for his children as he played the role of a grotesquely twisted god of his own making.

Then there were murderers with their own individual style. Richard Cottingham liked to wrap his victims into torso shapes and mutilate them—just for the sheer fun of it. And killers who killed for the sheer thrill of it, like Biegenwald, and like Reldan. Kuklinsky killed those who needed killing.

I

John List

Family Annihilator

Patricia Knew

ONE NIGHT IN THE FALL OF 1971, IN THE UPSCALE community of Westfield, New Jersey, John List gathered his family together for a meeting.

John List was a Lutheran, but was scrupulously observant. He insisted that his entire family be as obsessed with Lutheranism as he was. He was convinced they wouldn't go to heaven unless they were as devout as he was.

At the family meeting, List reviewed his rules and regulations and stressed that they be more attentive to them. John Jr., Patricia, Frederick, Helen, their mother, and Alma List, John's mother, all listened intently. They all went to church weekly whether they wanted to or not. They sang the hymns, although they found the melodies difficult. Their religiosity, however, was reserved for Sundays.

List's daughter wore trendy clothes, but he considered them too seductive. His wife, Helen, became exasperated with his domineering manner and turned to alcohol. Like all boys, his sons competed with their peer group for acceptance. Thus, they, too, engaged in the trendiest clothing and pop music. At home, List only permitted classical music on the radio, a source of aggravation and many complaints by his children.

Murder Announcement

On the night of the fateful meeting, List announced he was going to murder his family—all of them—except himself! He would do so, he said, to "save their souls." All except Patricia didn't believe him. List made threats all the time, especially the threat that they would go to hell if they didn't shape up. John Jr. wasn't surprised and neither were Helen, Alma, or Frederick. *'Now, he's finally flipped his cork,*' John Jr thought. They'd heard that warning before—over and over again.

List was not only a devout Lutheran, but a scrupulous one. He felt that his family was inattentive during the sermons at church. John Jr. was an avid soccer player, but was disinterested in studying the Bible. With all the appeals of secularism in the culture, List was extremely concerned they would succumb to the temptations of the devil and be condemned to hell.

While List's frequent threats were mostly ignored by the family, sixteen-year-old Patricia, was afraid—deathly afraid. In the fall of 1971, she went to her drama coach, Edwin Illiano whom she trusted, and told him the story. When Patricia started sobbing uncontrollably, Edwin became very concerned. Patricia wasn't given to such outbursts. Then he persuaded her that they should report this to the police.

They told the story to Officer John Moran of the Westfield Police Department. He was very open to listening to her complaint, but frankly had a hard time believing it. Moran also explained to them that the police couldn't take action on the basis of verbal threats unless some action accompanied them. Even an often-repeated threat wouldn't be sufficient to get a warrant or justify questioning List.

Then Illiano went to List's Lutheran pastor, Reverend Eugene Rehwinkel. Rehwinkel listened compassionately. The pastor knew List was extreme in his religious practice, but was convinced that List wouldn't commit the mortal sin of murder.

It was November 9, 1971. A cold crisp chill was in the air. John List had deliberately stayed home from work. He had an important task to accomplish. Full of anticipation, List went upstairs quietly. There was his wife, Helen, walking into their bedroom with a drink in her hand. She imbibed much too much, and—despite his prayers and his pleading—she wouldn't stop. She did tell him she was trying to cut back, but it never happened that way.

Without hesitation, he pulled his Colt .22 revolver out of his pocket, pointed it directly at the back of her head and squeezed the trigger. It was loud—louder than he thought it would be. She fell backward toward him. That surprised John and he leaped aside.

He dragged her into the room they called the "Ballroom." The room had originally been intended as such because the house used to be a beautiful mansion. The floor in that room was hardwood with a high polish to it, and a magnificent Tiffany-glass ceiling. Like all fashionable homes in the exclusive area of Westfield, New Jersey, the home had its own name: "Breezy Knoll." There was a wrought-iron gate that gave it the sinister look of a gothic novel. List glanced out the window then turned on the radio to a religious music station and turned the volume up high.

His mother, Alma, was upstairs in her attic room. She was hard-of-hearing, so she had no idea he was in the house. List had planned this out with military precision. One step at a time... he hadn't written his process out; he had it memorized. Perhaps she did hear something, because the elderly woman met him face-forward at the top of the stairs.

When she saw List's gun, she opened her mouth very, very wide and screamed. He shot her right above her left eye. Only a little bit of blood gushed out. The bullet went tearing toward the back of her head. This time, his victim did fall backward. Eerily, her mouth stayed wide open. She looked like fear itself.

Maybe she'd just gone shopping, as a bag was propped up next to her. It read, "O'Connor's"—a meat market. 'Typical,' sneered List... 'eating again.'

Patricia, who had poured her heart out to her drama coach, and thirteen-year-old Frederick, were still at school, but would be arriving home soon. John Jr, fifteen, was scheduled to play a soccer game after school. Clothes were strewn all over the house as his wife never stopped drinking long enough to do laundry. Apparently, the children were just as negligent. List had always reminded them to keep a tidy house. They didn't care, and now, neither did he.

Lunch

List never deviated from his daily routine. It was time for lunch, so he made himself a tuna fish sandwich, sat down at the disheveled kitchen table, and ate.

It was time to start the cover-up of his murderous scheme. Loose ends to take care of: cancelled the newspaper, cancelled the milk delivery. It was the 1970s and everyone had milk delivered to the door. Afterward, he rummaged through Mama Alma's papers and found her savings bonds. Then he grabbed the family checkbook and their bank statement. He knew the balance was a paltry amount... List was nearly bankrupt.

List was an accountant who was upwardly mobile like many skilled men his age. After a stint with the Xerox company in Rochester, he sought out a higher-paying position. He worked in the position of comptroller for a bank in Jersey City.

That's how the family was able to move to Westfield, a classy community. The taxes were high in Westfield, but he craved the prestige. It was expensive paying for the family in that community and he had to be very careful about his expenses. *"It's a great life, if you don't weaken."* But List *did* weaken. He couldn't afford to maintain his family there but was too embarrassed to say anything.

Domicile Preparations

He went to the bank, cashed in the bonds and closed the family bank account. Next, he went to the post office. He put in an order for them to hold his mail, explaining that he and his family were moving to North Carolina and didn't have a permanent address there yet. He'd let them know… but had no intention of doing so.

Murders of the Children

List heard the front door open and then Patricia came bouncing in. *'That foolish girl,'* he thought to himself smirking. *'She imagines she's going to become an actress. She'll go to hell if I don't stop her.'* Patricia walked into the kitchen, dropped her books on the kitchen table, but List was right there waiting for her. His gun was drawn. Her eyes went wide.

'Dad's announcement was coming true!'

25

List then swung her around. He wasn't going to mar Patricia's pretty face with a hideous gunshot wound. He calmly shot her in the back of her head. Catching her fall, he gently lowered her to the floor then dragged her by the feet into the ballroom. A trail of blood marked her path, so he wiped it up.

The door flew open again, and Frederick came stomping in. He threw down his backpack and walked toward the kitchen. His father was waiting for him. List stood still like a statue, pointing the gun at his son.

Frederick was startled. *"BLAM!"* The gun went off, and the boy crumbled to the floor.

List also dragged him into the ballroom and lined him up with his sister and mother. They were drenched in blood, so List grabbed a rag and wiped some of it up. When the wooden floor was cleaned off, he threw the rag in a garbage can.

He checked his watch. His eldest son, John Jr. was at Westfield High School playing in a soccer game. List drove over and sat through the entire game. He stared at the players, but wasn't really watching. His mind was moving a mile an hour.

Finally, John Jr. left the field and went to the locker room.

26

'*Almost time,*' List thought. '*Just a little longer and this will be over.*'

Upon arriving home, John Jr. heard the church music blaring from the ballroom. He tensed up. Somehow things didn't seem right. The atmosphere was heavy. It felt like Halloween somehow. No one seemed to be home. Mom was usually at the refrigerator or stove, and grandma would be at the kitchen table drinking tea. Dad had left a few scrunched-up napkins on the table, and there weren't any signs that supper was going to be made anytime soon.

"*Where's everybody?*" asked John Jr., turning to look at his father.

List pulled out his gun and took two steps toward young John. An emotional alarm squealed in John's mind, and he rushed toward his father, grabbing the gun. He hollered and the two of them struggled for possession of the gun. It went off a few times and John felt bullets sear through his thigh and arm.

Blood shot out, spattering on List and the wall behind him. They rolled around on the kitchen floor until List was able to wrench John Jr.'s head around. List then shot him in the back of his head. The hollering stopped. List watched, letting the image of

27

his dead son embed itself into his conscious mind. His bloodied body lay twisted near the kitchen table.

It was over. The deed was done.

"Where were those sleeping bags?" List asked himself. *'Let's tidy up here.'*

Then he remembered where they were and headed for the garage. He pulled them down from a shelf and shuffled back to the ballroom. One by one he placed the bodies of his wife and children into a sleeping bag. He covered each face with a dish towel. List realized with sadness that he couldn't bring his elderly mother downstairs to be with the family because she was too heavy.

Kneeling by the bodies, he prayed that God would forgive them all their transgressions during life. *'Surely now that they face their heavenly Father in judgement, they will see where they went wrong and repent, so they could enjoy paradise with God in heaven,'* List imagined.

He paraded around the house and cut his face out of every photograph he could find. The cops must not find out anything about him, and he was determined to avoid that. His presence in the family hadn't helped at all. He'd failed in his marriage; he'd failed to mold them into God-fearing people; he failed to support his family. They couldn't possibly afford to pay all the utilities and he couldn't afford to keep them clothed and have all the necessities of an upper middle-class life.

Next, he went to the schools his children attended and explained that the family was going to North Carolina to visit his wife's ailing mother. He would be in touch with the school prior to their return. List then went home quickly to double-check everything. All seemed to be in order—the order he wanted. Then he put all the lights on, went to the garage, drove to Kennedy International Airport and parked. He didn't take an airplane, though. That would throw the police off course.

Many men who kill, shoot themselves in the end, and List knew that. However, suicide was a sin and it deprived its sinner of heaven. It was the "unforgiveable sin," as the bible taught. List knew he would go to heaven, because he did this thing to save his family from being corrupted by the sinful world. He knew God would forgive him, and he would repent. Moreover, he still had time to start a new family—a family holy in the sight of God—and begin anew. The next time, he would do it right and that would make up for it.

A Long Month

The Lists weren't very social in the neighborhood, but they did have some connections in the community. Patricia List, who aspired to become an actress, missed the town rehearsal of the Tennessee Williams' play, "Streetcar." She had never missed a rehearsal. Her schoolmates, however, said she was away in North Carolina visiting their sick grandmother for a week, so no one was shocked. The only oversight they noted was the fact that Patricia didn't tell her classmates. They thought that was strange.

When a week passed and then another, the neighbors began to wonder. They had also noticed that the lights were on day and night at the List house. That seemed out of the ordinary because John List was very frugal. If he was going to be away, why hadn't he used timers?

Patricia's drama coach was extremely concerned. When he called her, there was never any answer, and he toyed with the idea of approaching the house to ask for her. Would she still be visiting in North Carolina? Why hadn't she called?

Then the neighbors began to notice that the lights on in the house were going out at an uneven pace. They were simply burning

List was sentenced to five consecutive life terms and died in prison in March of 2008. He was a man without remorse and no one had remorse for him.

II

Richard Kuklinski

The Iceman

STANLEY KUKLINSKI, RICHARD'S FATHER, WAS THE epitome of cruel. He beat his son for no reason; knocked him and hollered just for the sake of letting out pent-up feelings. As a result, Richard Kuklinski hated dogs and cats, and it thrilled him to torture them.

When his father came home, which wasn't often, he would be violently drunk and regularly took his anger on all three of his sons. When his younger brother was nine, Kuklinski's father beat him so badly the boy died. After that, Kuklinski's father deserted the family. The man was a bastard and Kuklinski often wished he had murdered him while he'd had the chance.

Kuklinski's mother wasn't much better. She had a hang-up about strict corporal punishment and beat him with broom handles. Kuklinski never experienced the love of his family.

The Edison Bridge

The Edison Bridge spans the Raritan River—a brown, heavily polluted river that connects the industrial city of Woodbridge, New Jersey, with Sayreville, a southern Jersey town. Cars stop on the Edison Bridge all the time, and some even commit suicide there by heaving themselves over the edge.

Richard Kuklinski used the Raritan as a body dump for Charley Lane. Kuklinski hated Charley. Ever since he and Kuklinski were teens, Charley teased him and bullied him unmercifully. In 1948, Kuklinski had had enough. He duped Charley into meeting him at a bar, got him drunk, threw him in the back seat of his truck. He considered throwing him over the Edison Bridge, but changed his mind and pulled over into the tall straw-like grasses under the bridge. He dragged Charley out of the truck and struck him with his truck and a wooden dowel.

'*Better not leave any identification,*' he thought to himself. So he bent down and cut off Charley's fingertips. They bled like hell, which surprised him. Then he got a pair of oily pliers from his truck and wrenched out all his teeth. Grabbing his legs, Kuklinski dragged Charley across the swampy grasses and threw him in the truck bed. Taking off at a slow pace, he pulled over and heaved good ol' Charley over a railing, dumping him into the mud below.

And just like that, his red-hot temper calmed. Kuklinski kept waiting for more of a reaction, like joy or sorrow, perhaps. But he felt nothing... nothing at all. It was a job, and it was done. Just that and nothing more.

Linda Kuklinski

Kuklinski married a girl named Linda, that he got pregnant. They had two children together, but Kuklinski really lacked the ability to like them very much at all. He never beat them, though. He wasn't going to repeat what his father had done.

When their relationship cooled, Linda started seeing another man. Kuklinski's brother, Joseph, told him about the affair. Kuklinski headed to the motel where he beat the boyfriend, Sammy James, within an inch of his life.

38

Turning to Linda, who declared, *"If you weren't the mother of my sons..."* He hesitated, then pulled out his knife and cut off her nipples. She screeched and passed out.

They never saw each other again.

Barbara Kuklinski

Kuklinski later met a woman named Barbara. She found him exciting, and he liked to lavish her with gifts. She became pregnant by him, but also started to notice that he had violent fits of anger.

She told him she was ambiguous about their relationship, Kuklinski pulled a knife out of his sock and stabbed her in her back, saying that if he couldn't have her; no one would. It was a superficial wound, but Barbara felt trapped.

Kuklinski often beat Barbara. However, he was extremely changeable and would sometimes treat her to fine restaurants and dancing. Barbara was deathly afraid of him and did not want to displease him. She privately referred to him either as the "good Richard," or the "bad Richard," as his mood swings were violent and unpredictable.

Barbara and he had three children—Merrick, Christin, and Dewayne. Despite his explosive nature, Kuklinski never beat his children. Visions of his father's brutality cured him of that.

Barbara knew he had snakes crawling around in his head, and had businesses which he would never discuss. She knew better than to ask him, but she was always an uncomfortable and anxiety-prone woman.

The Final Round

The summer of 1979, Carmine Genovese, brother of crime boss Vito Genovese had heard about Kuklinski and knew the young man was earning his way up the ranks in a crime family.

Kuklinski would never be a "made man," though. A "made man" was one who had murdered for the mob, but he had to be Italian in order to merit the term "made man." Kuklinski was a Polack, but what did he care? "Independent contractor" would do as far as he was concerned.

Sometimes the mob hired outside the family if they needed a hit man who knew how to keep his mouth shut. Kuklinski knew how. He called his private crew, "Coming Up Roses," and spread the word around. The name had a ring to it, and told the story.

One evening Carmine Genovese handed Kuklinski a photo, saying, *"Take care of him."* The photo was of a non-descript man getting into a Lincoln. *"You want the work?"* asked Genovese.

"Yeah, absolutely," Kuklinski responded.

"Good. This gotta' happen quick, understand? Anything goes wrong, you call me. We own the cops here, okay?"

Kuklinski called his guys and they drove toward a waterfront bar called the "Final Round." A Lincoln stopped at the light and the car was right next to theirs. Kuklinski leaned over and told his partner, John Wheeler to shoot the man. Wheeler froze. Sometimes that happens when novice killers see their "mark."

The mark got away, and Kuklinski told Wheeler he'd do it himself. Kuklinski followed the Lincoln to the bar. Finally, the mark parked, got out, and went inside. Now came the long wait. Finally, after nearly two hours, the mark came out. He was staggering. That was good. It was raining slightly and it was dark. That was also good.

Kuklinsky took Wheeler's gun and approached the Lincoln. The window was still open, so he took out the gun, shoved it up to the guy's head and shot him just above his left ear. Brains and blood

41

spattered on the window of the passenger seat. The man slid down the seat and Kuklinski ambled back to their car.

"Man, Rich, you're cold as ice!" commented Wheeler. Kuklinski smirked.

They returned to Genovese for their pay, which was a mere fifty dollars each, but it was a start, Kuklinski told Wheeler and his other pal, Jack Dubrowski. Carmine was extremely impressed with their rapid response and gave them a lot of work.

In the spring of 1979, Genovese asked Kuklinski for a special treatment for his next hit. The mark was a loud-mouthed car salesman who gave a friend of Genovese's a bad deal. Genovese said he wanted the guy to "suffer," and he wanted Kuklinski to bring back a souvenir.

Kuklinski went to the dealership on the pretext of buying a car. When it was time for the test drive, Kuklinski took the vehicle into some nearby woods, while the man protested. Kuklinski pulled the car over near a tree and tied the salesman to it. The man howled and screeched as Kuklinski took out an axe from his jacket, and hacked the man's legs off. The man fainted as blood gushed out of his legs like red waterfalls. Kuklinski then cut off the man's fingers.

Kuklinski thought about bringing Genovese the fingers, but mulled it a bit. For his final feat, Kuklinski decided to outdo himself. Taking the axe, he lifted it high, and chopped the man's head clean off his body. He wrapped it in the paper mats car dealers put on the floors of the show cars.

Genovese broke out into a total smile when he saw that. *"This Kuklinski guy is going to be an invaluable asset,"* thought Genovese.

Genovese's enforcer, DeMeo hired Kuklinski to do a few "jobs" for him during the 1970s. He was to make "collections," meaning he was to collect payments from people who had taken out loans. If they failed to pay, Kuklinski beat them. In cases when the offense was repeated, he killed them. Some he shot clean straight in the back of the head; others he strangled, and then shoved their bodies into an oil drum and set it on fire. Kuklinsky delighted in hearing the crackling sound made when the fat on their bodies was consumed by the flames.

The Commission

In order to prevent encroachments on each other territories, and to organize the mob, the heads of the five crime families consulted each other on events that might impact their respective businesses to avoid gang wars.

The five families were: the Genovese family under Vito Geneovese; the Lucchese family under Tommy Lucchese, the Colombo family under Joseph Colombo, the Gambino family under Carlo Gambino, and the Bonanno family under Joe Bonanno.

Carmine Galante was one of the Genovese soldiers. He controlled all the drug routes between Italy, Canada, and New York, and later from New York to New Jersey. Galante had worked for the Genovese family, but then he was allowed to become the underboss of the Bonanno family.

Galante had been in prison when the families let Gambino assume control of the route. Galante wanted the route back once he got out of prison. Galante got greedy and decided to grab some of the Gambino narcotics trade for himself. One by one, Galante killed Gambino's henchmen.

The Criminal Commission met. Since the Genovese family had sponsored Carmine Galante, they felt embarrassed at Galante's behavior. This was unheard of. Because Galante was then working as the underboss of Joe Bonanno, the Genovese teams asked for his permission to put out a contract on Galante. With a nod, Bonanno approved. The families didn't want that young upstart to set up his own narcotics empire right under their noses.

DeMeo contacted Kuklinski, and gave him the job.

On July 12, 1979, Galante and two bodyguards walked into Joe and Mary's Italian Restaurant in downtown New York.

Kuklinski's crew pulled up in their Lincoln, stopped and leaned out their windows. They covered their faces with hoods. Kuklinski stood squarely in front of Galante and opened fire. He shot out Galante's left eye, and riddled his chest with bullets. Blood ran over the edge of the street. His bodyguard, Leonard Coppola, was killed outright.

Mister Softee

Robert Pronge, a former Special Forces veteran, was one of Kuklinski's mentors. Pronge did some surveillance work for the Gambino family, using his Mister Softee truck as a cover. In addition, if there was someone Gambino needed done away with, Pronge, with his knowledge of explosives and chemicals, could also act as a hit man like Kuklinski.

About Pronge, Kuklinski once said, *"He taught me a lot, but he was extremely crazy. He'd go into these neighborhoods, sell ice cream to the kids, then maybe kill one of their fathers."* Pronge also taught Kuklinski about filling a nasal spray with cyanide and shooting it into the mouths of victims. It was a very painful death.

One Dead Cop

Kuklinski met some of the members of the Gambino crime family, and his reputation for getting the job done was well-known. In March of 1980, Kuklinski got a contract from a messenger for a big man in the family, Sammy "the Bull" Gravano. He was in jail at the time on a narcotics charge, but had a way of getting jobs done from jail. Although "the Bull" had all the local cops in Bergen county and New York "on the take," "the Bull" had a "beef" against a certain cop, Peter Calabro.

"The Bull" didn't trust Calabro to keep family secrets, because sensitive information was reaching the ears of the FBI. Perhaps as a warning to prevent Calabro from leaking information to the FBI, Calabro's wife drowned under mysterious circumstances. However, that didn't keep Calabro from "mouthing off." If the Gambino's were imprisoned, Calabro might try to hone in on the family business. Therefore, he had to be "whacked" (killed).

Kuklinski, the guy who says nothing and knows less about the people, was hired to kill him. Kuklinski parked his big, white van along a street in North Bergen, and waited for Calabro to drive by. The street was narrow, so no one would be moving fast.

As Calabro, in his vehicle, approached Kuklinski's parked van, Kuklinski leaped out. With his sawed-off shot gun Kuklinski pulled the trigger. Calabro's head flew off his torso and was flung against the passenger window. Kuklinski headed back to his van and took off. The tires squealed loudly when he left. Job done.

The Foolish Partners

John Wheelwright and Jack Dubrowski liked this new life of crime they had embarked on due to Kuklinski's connection with Carmine Genovese. They met many of Genovese's men, including Albert Parenti, one of Genovese's made men. The Genovese crowd loved poker, as there was a lot of money in those games.

Kuklinski's partners, Wheelwright and Dubrowski, thought it would be a good idea to raid one of their poker games and steal the money. They went into the back room wearing bandannas and raked in thousands of dollars. Everybody knew it was them anyway, as they were the only guys who knew about the game.

Kuklinski, on the other hand, knew nothing about this bold robbery. If he had, he would have warned his partners. Kuklinski was smart and knew that mob guys always take out their revenge for betrayal. Kuklinski got a call from Parenti, asking for a "sit-down," which is the term for an important meeting.

Kuklinski drove to Phil's restaurant in Jersey City, and spoke to Parenti.

Parenti told Kuklinski about the robbery, adding that he knew Kuklinski was not involved.

Kuklinski was horrified when he heard the story but tried to intercede for the waywardness of his imbecilic partners, saying he would make sure they would never try something like that again.

Parenti didn't care about getting restitution, though. The cardinal rule was: NO ONE ROBS THE MOB. Parenti looked at Kuklinski eye-to-eye. *"They gotta' go. That's it. You do it or we do it, capice?"*

Kuklinski had to kill them. If he didn't he'd be killed and he knew it. Kuklinski's stomach wrenched up inside and his face went white. Nevertheless, Kuklinski did his duty.

Dubrowski was at his girlfriend's house when Kuklinski tracked him down. The murder was short. Then he met up with John Wheelwright in Jersey City and—as they were walking—Kuklinski pulled him into an alley and shot him in the back of the head. He knew that word would get back to Genovese if he left the body right there near the city street.

On DeMeo

Roy DeMeo was a "made man" with the Gambino Crime Family. Kuklinski had few vices, but he did gamble, and gambled heavily. In the early '70s, he failed to pay a debt to loan shark, Roy DeMeo, filled the role of enforcer, so he confronted Kuklinksi.

Kuklinski promised he'd pay the money back. When he turned casually toward the elevator to leave, DeMeo's men drew their guns on him. *"So, tough guy, you want to die, you want to fuckin' die?"* they asked. They didn't shoot, though. Instead, they brutally beat Kuklinski. It was his first and last warning.

In reality, Kuklinski had a gun with him—just a little Derringer—but he didn't dare try to pull it on those guys, knowing he was outnumbered and outmuscled. A week after he got out of

49

the hospital, Kuklinski boldly strolled into the Gemini Club DeMeo owned and paid the debt in full with interest.

DeMeo was astonished at Kuklinski's courage, because no one paid in person. Kuklinski then told DeMeo that the two thugs DeMeo sent to beat up Kuklinski were stealing from the mob, and from each other.

DeMeo liked Kuklinski after that revelation. He felt he was a real "stand-up" guy. DeMeo also revealed the fact that he knew Kuklinski was carrying a gun, as a matter of fact, and respected the fact that he didn't use it.

Kuklinski then shared with DeMeo that he had a pornographic business on the side, along with another business that sold pirated videotapes. They decided to work the city together.

Kuklinski did a lot of contract killings for DeMeo and Genovese. He tried to vary his methods of killing each time to throw investigators off. Besides, it was fun, and added variety. He was really fond of breaking up bodies and stuffing them into oil drums. One could take the leg, bend it the wrong way and feel a sense of sheer delight to hear the tendons rip and the bones crack. Bodies had unnatural bumps and protrusions in them by the time he was done. He didn't like blood that much; it was messy.

Cyanide was bloodless so that was another favorite of Kuklinski's. He had learned from Mr. Softee how to convert it into a spray, so administration was simple. Kuklinski felt a sense of satisfaction when he saw guys fold in half with excruciating cramps and loud moans. The beauty of the cocaine spray was that it was difficult to trace in a body a few days after death.

Malliband: R.I.P.

It was now February 1980. George Malliband was an old hunting buddy of Kuklinski's. He was a heavy gambler and got into trouble with DeMeo. When Malliband begged Kuklinski to intercede, Kuklinski did so, and DeMeo extended a loan to Malliband for thirty-five thousand dollars at a "friend's rate." Kuklinski then told Malliband that he had better pay off as soon as possible. *"That guy is dangerous,"* Kuklinski warned Malliband.

Malliband not only owed money to the Jersey mob guys; he also owed money in Las Vegas. Malliband then used the thirty-five thousand to pay his Las Vegas debts, but didn't have enough yet to pay back DeMeo. After begging Kuklinski for an extension, he did get one. He made a few payments on the recast loan, but then stopped. DeMeo came back at Kuklinski heavy and strong.

51

Malliband was desperate and again begged Kuklinski to help him.

"Look, I can't help you," Kuklinski told him. *"You swore on your word of honor, on all your relatives that you'd do the right thing. DeMeo—you can't fuck around with this guy. He's fucking dangerous."*

Malliband then made the fatal error of turning against Kuklinski. On their way home, Malliband started an argument with Kuklinski during which he threatened Kuklinski's family.

Kuklinski pulled his van off Route 46, took out a .38 revolver from his pocket and shot him squarely in the chest five times. NO ONE THREATENS HIS FAMILY AND LIVES! Kuklinski removed an oil drum from inside the van, broke Malliband's legs and forced the body into the drum. The drum was eventually found in the back of Chemitex plant in Jersey City.

The investigators who found the twisted body also found twenty-seven thousand dollars with him. Malliband had had the money, but wanted to keep it for himself.

Masgay: Freeze the Nuisance

Kuklinski set up his outfit like a junior-size mafia, only he was forced to run it with undisciplined men. Kuklinski spent years developing an enterprise with Pronge, a.k.a. Mister Softee, selling pirated videotapes from points of distribution. It was doing extremely well. However, in July of 1981, problems developed.

Kuklinski was famous for his violent temper, and often flew off in fits of rage. That happened in his dealings with Louis Masgay. Masgay was a middle-man in the videotape operation. He insatiably bought hundreds of blank tapes from Kuklinski's supply man, Phil Solimene. Masgay was a "nudge," who nagged and nagged Kuklinski and the boys whenever he came by Solimene's store to buy blank tapes.

Kuklinski couldn't stand him. Masgay was disorganized and never gave Solimene advance warning. He would just pop in anytime. *"When will you have more tapes? I got cash money,"* he would always say. *"No questions asked."*

On July 1, 1981, Masgay came rushing into the store breathless. After informing Solimene he needed a huge amount of new blank tapes, he said that the money for them was hidden in the side panel of his van. Solimene called Kuklinski to let him know. There was something big planned.

Kuklinski didn't want to work with Masgay anymore, because of all the poor planning. He was tired of it. When he heard about the money, though, Kuklinski arrived at Solimene's store in less than an hour.

"Where is he?" asked Kuklinski.

"In the john," replied Solimene.

With three giant steps Kuklinski stepped to the back of the store, and tore open the bathroom door. There was Masgay sitting on the toilet. He looked up in shock. Kuklinski aimed his .22 and shot Masgay in the left eye and then between both eyes. The bullets tore through his head opening up a hole in the back of his skull. A red puddle spread over the tiled floor. The huge hole in Masgay's head had discolored mush inside. Kuklinski took the money and got rid of Masgay's truck.

Kuklinski apologized to Phil Solimene for the mess. People, including Masgay's relatives, knew he was going to Solimene's, so they had to disguise the time of death and tell them that Masgay never arrived. Kuklinski didn't want to involve his friend, Phil

Solimene, so he approached Robert Pronge—"Mister Softee." Did Pronge have access to a meat freezer? That way, the body would be out of Solimene's store and he could also throw off the county coroner in ascertaining the date of Masgay's death.

Pronge obliged Kuklinski, so he first put Masgay's body into his Mister Softee truck to take to the large freezer. He bent up Masgay's body tightly until the joints crunched. The guy had been in the process of defecating when Kuklinski shot him, so it was quite a mess and it stank. They dragged the body to the large freezer and covered the body with plastic, throwing it on the freezer floor. That's how Richard Kuklinski got the nickname the "Ice Man."

Mister Softee Melts

In 1984, Pronge called Kuklinski, and invited him to take a ride with him to Runnymede, New Jersey—a town down in Camden county, South Jersey. That's where Pronge's route now was. While he and Kuklinski were in his truck, Pronge asked Kuklinski to get rid of his wife and son. They were going to testify in court that Pronge had beat them.

Kuklinski refused, saying he didn't get involved in domestic matters.

Pronge was furious, and couldn't talk Kuklinski into murdering his ex-wife and son. Pronge was a man full of hate and vengeance. During their car ride, Kuklinski discovered that Pronge planned on poisoning a nearby community reservoir in order to kill off a family he didn't like. Kuklinski realized he was dealing with a madman. There was no way Kuklinski wanted anyone to connect him with a man so depraved and so evil.

'Pronge shouldn't be allowed to live,' thought Kuklinski. He then had Pronge pull off the road on the pretext he wanted a couple of cones. As soon as Pronge bent over the ice cream machine, Kuklinski took out his derringer and shot him in his chest twice. What a bloody mess it made of the wooden boarded floor of the Mister Softee truck! Its time it would reek. Kuklinski smiled and wondered how long it would take anyone to go looking for some free ice cream.

Phil Hoffman, Pharmacist

It was tough making a living by running a small drugstore. Hoffman, a trained pharmacist, noted that he sold a lot of Tagamet, a prescription drug to treat ulcers. He knew that he could make a huge profit if he could get a hold of the drug at a low price.

Hoffman knew a lot of people on the streets who told him about a variety store in Paterson that sold stolen items from their backroom.

Kuklinski also knew about this store and was hanging out there and met Hoffman. Hoffman could see that Kuklinski seemed to know the owners and the store personnel. Hoffman approached Kuklinski, and told him that he had a deal to make. If Kuklinski could provide Hoffman with a couple cases of Tagamet, he could make twenty-five thousand dollars. *'What a deal that would be!'* thought Kuklinski.

Kuklinski agreed to meet Hoffman in the back of a warehouse, promising the goods on April 29, 1982. That day, Hoffman came slinking into the building. It was loaded with hijacked items like VCR players, speakers, and even tires. Kuklinski signaled to him and waved. Hoffman came close to Kuklinski and pulled out the cash—twenty-seven thousand dollars.

Kuklinski grabbed the cash and stuffed it in his pocket. Then he slammed Hoffman into the wall and told him it was a ruse. Hoffman didn't have a chance to respond. Kuklinski pulled his gun out and shoved it under Hoffman's chin, squeezing the trigger. Hoffman slid down the wall, jerking his head back and forth frantically. He grabbed his throat and threw his head back, banging it over and over against a store shelf.

Kuklinski pulled the trigger again, but the lousy gun jammed. Then he threw himself into Hoffman, wrestled him to the floor and beat his face with a tire iron he brought "just in case." Hoffman's head swelled and blood gushed out of his nostrils. Kuklinski choked him. Hoffman was dead.

Now, for the body. With any murder, the biggest problem was getting rid of the corpse. Kuklinski dragged the body out back, bent it up in a fetal position, and heaved it into a barrel along with some instant cement he'd had in the back of his truck.

After dark, he drove to Harry's Corner, a luncheonette he knew about in South Hackensack. He rolled the barrel out of his truck bed, and added some water to it from the standpipe alongside the building. Then he tucked it in near the back of an alley.

He stopped at the luncheonette a few times after that to see if the barrel was gone. He was just curious. After weeks had passed, it was finally missing. None of the customers ever talked about it. Kuklinski never knew what happened to it. Who would want a dead man in a barrel?

The Gang

Kuklinski didn't always work as a hit man or a robber. Through Carmine Genovese, he worked at Swiftline trucking company in Paterson. That wasn't Kuklinski's preferred line of work, but he discovered he could hijack trucks, and sell the merchandise from one of the Paterson warehouses. Genovese usually gave him a lead to score big. In those cases, he gave Genovese half the profit.

Percy House, Gary Smith, and Daniel Deppner were now the new members of his gang. They called him "Big Rich." In northern Hudson County, over forty burglaries occurred in a five-block area. All the purloined items went to the Paterson warehouse and their guys got in touch with buyers on the streets.

In 1982, police nabbed Percy House, one of Kuklinski's gang members. Figuring that House would rat to the cops, Kuklinski called Deppner and Smith and ordered them to go into hiding. The joint he selected was the York Motel, on Route 3, close to the Lincoln Tunnel. It was famous for its prostitutes and should keep Kuklinski's guys entertained while they were holed up.

Deppner and Smith got a room there, but Smith—the imbecile of the bunch—decided this was a good time to visit his sister. Smith's foolhardiness concerned Kuklinski. He realized he'd have to eliminate Smith when he got back.

Gary Smith Had to go

Kuklinski had it well-planned. In December 1982, when Smith came back, Kuklinski sent Deppner for a take-out meal from a hamburger joint and had it brought it back to the motel room. Kuklinski then laced the burger with cyanide and both of them waited. Smith complained about a sick stomach, and heaved up in the bathroom. Much to the shock of Deppner and Kuklinski, Smith came out, lay down on the bed and snapped on the TV.

"I don't 'frickin' believe this," whispered an exasperated Kuklinski. *"Choke him with a lamp cord, Danny!"* commanded Kuklinski. Deppner leaped on top of Smith and pulled the cord tight around Smith's neck. Smith gagged and wiggled a few times, then sank down on the bed. Dead.

There was always the problem with body disposal in a city. Kuklinski and Deppner stuffed Smith's body between the box spring and the mattress in their room and fled in the middle of the

60

night. The whole motel reeked of dirt and grime anyway and was overrun with roaches, no chance of finding it anytime soon.

Kuklinski was right. A few more guests rented that room before the decomposed body was discovered by its smell. It took them a month.

Deppner's Last Meal: Burnt Beans

Daniel Deppner was now a liability because he knew too much and Percy House was under protective custody, so he might "spill the beans." No doubt Percy House would talk his fool head off to get a lighter sentence. Deppner wasn't the "sharpest knife in the drawer," so to speak, so it never occurred to him that he was going to be Kuklinski's next victim.

Kuklinski did like Deppner, so he put off killing him for a while. Deppner was a good "gopher" kind of guy who'd get Kuklinksi anything he wanted.

He planned this murder out carefully. Kuklinski's daughter, Merrick, had a fiancé, Rich Patterson, who lived in Bergenfield. Bergenfield was a low-class but neatly-kept development of immigrant families mostly "transplants" from New York City. Kuklinski's hometown, Dumont, was the next town over.

61

Kuklinski took Rich Patterson aside one day, and told him that Deppner was in serious trouble with the police and needed to hide out for a few days. Upon Kuklinski's behest, Deppner ate supper there with Patterson, rather than go out to a restaurant where Deppner might be seen.

Rich Patterson worked on weekends and was out of the house. Kuklinski went over there and heated up some canned vegetables for Deppner and himself. Kuklinski was a lousy cook, but he managed to heat up some kidney beans, and even though he burned them, Kuklinski insisted Deppner eat them anyway. Why let food go to waste?

Unknown to Deppner, Kuklinski had laced the beans with cyanide. After supper, Deppner developed pink spots on his face—signs of cyanide poisoning. Next, he bent over in pain, and curled up in a fetal position. Kuklinski then heaped his body.

When Paterson arrived home that mild day in May of 1983, he was horrified. Deppner's face was pasted into an eerie grimace.

Kuklinski then told Paterson that when he stepped out, the cops or somebody broke in and killed Deppner. *"It had to do with Deppner's legal problems,"* Kuklinski remarked.

Kuklinski told Paterson they'd better hide the body. If it was reported to the cops, they might get accused of harboring a fugitive. Clinton Avenue was the next main north-south road and it was a heavily wooded area. *'Perfect for a body dump.'*

They wrapped Deppner up in a few green garbage bags, dragged the body into the woods and left it there.

Along Came Kane

Pat Kane was a prominent investigator for the New Jersey State Police. In 1985, the murders of various low life criminals that danced in and out of the system ended up in the files and were piped along to Pat Kane. Among the cases were that of Daniel Deppner, Gary Smith, Masgay, Hoffman, and Malliband. Their names had frequently shown up on Kane's desk for various crimes like robbery, murder, and assault. Now all of them were in the morgue.

Most of them died of unusual circumstances—Deppner died of cyanide poisoning. Smith's decomposed body was found under a motel room mattress. Louis Masgay's stiff body was found in Rockland County, New York. He had been partially frozen but thawed out. That's how the police were finally able to identify his body. Paul Hoffman was a known dealer selling prescription drugs.

63

He was found with half his head blown off in a mob warehouse in Paterson.

George Malliband made the fatal mistake of threatening Kuklinski's family. No one—but no one—threatens his family and lives. Kuklinski himself, though, had his own moments of violence against his wife. Kuklinski, in his unpredictable fits of physical rage, broke her nose more than once, and was also beaten by him. Occasionally, he did change like Mr. Hyde into Dr. Jekyll and took her out to eat to classy restaurants, and sent her flowers.

There was some limited circumstantial evidence to link Kuklinski to the murders of those individuals, but Pat Kane needed more. In the interest of doing that, he set up a sting operation. Kane recruited a friend of Kuklinski—Phil Solimene—who was also a supplier for Kuklinski's burglary operation. Kane threatened Solimene with prison, but said his sentence would be short if Solimene could put Kane in touch with an undercover agent who would play the role of a mafia-type of character.

The agent's name was Dominic Polifrone. Polifrone was wired with a hidden microphone. Solimene arranged a meeting between Polifrone and Kuklinski. As they socialized, Kuklinski bragged about doing away with people using cyanide. That provided Kane with sufficient evidence to arrest Kuklinski, but they arranged one last "deal" with him just to be sure they'd collected enough evidence.

The Big Sting Falls Flat

Polifrone told Kuklinski that he had a big deal in the works— an exchange of cocaine for cyanide. As per Kuklinski's request, the undercover cop brought him a sample of the "cyanide." However, Kuklinski tried it out on a dog, and when it didn't work, he didn't show up to close the deal.

Kane and his force then tracked Kuklinski and set up a roadblock. As he was pulling out of his driveway to bring his wife to the doctor, the cops swooped in. The officers dragged both Kuklinski and his wife from the car.

It took eight officers to bring him to the ground, as he was very agitated about their rough treatment of Barbara. Barbara herself was charged with possession of a deadly weapon since a gun was found stashed under the passenger seat.

The Trial

It was difficult getting first-hand evidence regarding the murders Kuklinski had committed. However, Paul Kane and his team were able to solicit the aid of Rich Patterson, Kuklinski's daughter's fiancé.

When Kuklinski had his pal, Daniel Deppner, stay there, blood evidence found under the carpet connected the killing of Daniel Deppner with Kuklinski. Because Kuklinski's wife was charged with gun possession, Kane promised her mercy if she also testified. She then admitted in court that she heard her husband talk about the murder of Gary Smith.

Forensic teams were also able to establish that two of Kuklinski's victims died of cyanide poisoning.

During the course of the trial, Kuklinski once held up his fingers in the make-believe gesture of shooting his defender, Frank Neal. That, along with Kuklinski's smugness, served to help persuade the jurors.

Realizing his weakness was his love for his wife, the District Attorney indicated he would drop the gun charges against Barbara Kuklinski altogether if he confessed to the murders he was on trial for: those of Gary Smith, Phil Hoffman, Louis Masgay, Daniel Deppner, and George Malliband. He had killed others, but the prosecutors lacked sufficient evidence to land a conviction. Kuklinski confessed to the murders of the five men and was convicted.

The jury sentenced him to four consecutive life terms and he wouldn't be eligible for parole until that time was served. The time amounted to one hundred eleven years, he wouldn't live to be paroled.

Kuklinski died at New Jersey State Prison of a rare blood disorder in 2006.

III

Richard Biegenwald

The Thrill Killer

RICHARD BIEGENWALD WANTED TO EXPERIENCE the inside and outside of death in an intimate way. Unfortunately, so did the medical examiners who were required to autopsy the remains of the poorly discarded bodies he left behind. One was a girl of seventeen, whose body was buried under wet mud in parts and pieces. One of the New Jersey investigators, Robert Lucia, was compelled to witness the examination of her body.

"It was one of the worst things I've ever smelled," he said. *"She wasn't found for three to four weeks, and part of her that was on the pillow was nothing but maggots."*

The bodies they found had been chopped in pieces, with rotten meat torn off the bones. The killer clearly enjoyed the gruesome look of the bloodied, broken limbs of once-beautiful girls.

"Have Gun – Am Traveling"

Biegenwald's inaugural experience with murder happened in 1958, when he took the Staten Island Ferry to Bayonne, New Jersey. He managed to get a hold of a shot gun—a twelve-gage J.C. Higgins. This first murder was just for practice. The victim was Stephen Sadlowski, a shopkeeper, who also happened to be a part-time prosecutor in Manhattan.

The two of them had a penchant for drama, so Biegenwald's pal, James Sparnroft, put blackface on himself. Biegenwald was disguised as the TV character, Paladin, a pitted-faced cowboy who carried the card: *"Have Gun—Will Travel."* Biegenwald had a new card made up similar to that one: *"Have Gun—Am Traveling."*

Biegenwald stomped into a store while Sadlowski was tallying up for the night. Without flinching, he aimed his rifle for Sadlowski's stomach and squeezed the trigger. After the shooting, Biegenwald stole a 1952 cream-colored Mercury sedan and drove like a madman into Maryland.

69

Cops followed him and had a shootout with him in Salisbury. He was extradited to New Jersey, as that's where the murder occurred. That same year, he was convicted of murder and given a life sentence. However, in 1975, he was paroled for good behavior. That was a mistake.

Biegenwald was the kind of person who could function well in the structured environment of a prison, but couldn't handle freedom. He had already been in a structured locked institution before—the State Training School for Boys in New York—but reverted once he was freed. After he had completed his term there, Biegenwald kept a low profile. That was temporary. He simply had to give into his baser instincts again. When he was in Brooklyn in 1977, he spotted this lovely young girl walking down the sidewalk. He became aroused so he followed her, watching her sweet little fanny wiggle as she walked.

He grabbed her, pulled her into an alley. Police suspected that he raped her. There were no eyewitnesses, because he was often seen in that area, following young women. The rape went unreported.

Killing of John Petrone

John Petrone was one of Biegenwald's prison buddies. He was released and lived with his mother in a motel in Point Pleasant in 1978. Biegenwald hated him because Petrone was a police informant. Biegenwald ran into him at an auction where he purchased an old police car. This was his big chance to get back at the guy for being a rat.

Pretending to be friendly, Biegenwald suggested the two of them go out to the abandoned airport in Flemington and do some target practice. Petrone agreed.

They knocked off a few rounds into tin cans. At the end of the match, Biegenwald pointed his gun directly at Petrone. Petrone thought he was kidding until Biegenwald let out four shots point-blank into Petrone's skull. He stuffed Petrone's body in the trunk of the car and drove all the way to a wildlife park in Jackson. It was a relatively deserted area and his body was found many years later, but without its jawbone.

Rape Charge

In 1980, he was charged with rape and picked up in Brooklyn, New York. However, the victim failed to identify him in a lineup and he was released. Her name wasn't released publicly.

Stint at Brooklyn House of Detention

Shortly thereafter, the cops received a call from his parole officer. Biegenwald was required to have regular meetings with him from his 1958 conviction, but he had missed several appointments. That gave Detective Robert Miller sufficient reason to pick him up.

Biegenwald was detained briefly at the Brooklyn House of Detention. While there, his girlfriend from school, Dianne Merseles, came to visit him and they were married in June, much to the horror of her parents.

When he was released from detention, he and his new wife moved to Point Peasant Beach, New Jersey, to a rooming house. When Biegenwald and his new wife were able to pull enough money together by holding various jobs, they moved to Asbury Park and rented a first floor apartment in an old Victorian house. The landlord took a liking to them and permitted Biegenwald to collect his rents for him, and paid him a percentage of the rental income.

He also picked up a job waxing floors for a local supermarket at night.

Biegenwald liked the boardwalk in Asbury and enjoyed sitting on a bench watching young girls going by in their tiny swimsuits. In 1980, he spotted lovely, eighteen-year-old Anna Olesiewicz and dragged her under the boardwalk where he caressed her skin but didn't rape her. He ended up shooting her and then carrying her body to his vehicle and drove to Ocean Township. There was plenty of scrub brush behind the beach dunes, so he stashed her body behind a fast food restaurant.

In Asbury Park, Biegenwald befriended Dherran Fitzgerald, an ex-con. Once on his own at his night job, he and Dherran planned capers together. They robbed the stores and sold the goods. They were careful not to take so much that it would be missed. His wife, Dianne, worked for a pharmacy in Oakhurst. It was said that she was friendly, but Biegenwald had a dark personality. He seemed distant and didn't invite conversation.

During the days, Biegenwald and his pal, Dherran, hung out at the Asbury Park beach teasing and taunting teen girls.

The Weapons Cache

At their Asbury Park house, the landlord had a small basement apartment. He rented it out to a young woman named Theresa Smith. Despite the fact that Biegenwald normally wasn't that friendly, he did have a soft spot for her. She was naïve and simple. He decided to take her "under his wing" and influence her. She helped him spot new victims and he paid her for that "service."

He also had plans to rob banks and recruited Dherran along with Theresa to help him out with grandiose plans to make a lot of money. He and Dherran schemed and plotted to invent weapons and create a kind of black market to sell them. The two of them managed to obtain designs for making primitive guns using a drill press and a grinder—which Dherran stole. They found plans for converting cocaine into an inhalable gas and put together the device. Dherran was skilled in mechanics, and knew enough about it to use the equipment they collected. Dherran and he also accumulated automatic pistols and ammunition, including a machine gun, rifles, and pipe bombs.

Biegenwald created a hiding spot in his apartment wall where they stashed some of their equipment and goods. He also kept a poisonous snake there—a puff adder—along with a few marijuana plants. Dianne Biegenwald was able to steal some pills from the pharmacy where she worked and let him have them. They could be used to render a person unconscious. Dianne, however, wasn't aware of all the weapons he harbored.

Mom's House

Having grown up on Staten Island, New York, Biegenwald often visited home. His mother, was in her mid-sixties, and lived alone, after having divorced her abusive husband. She lived in the Richmond section of Staten Island, not far from the ferry that traveled to and from Bayonne in New Jersey. Biegenald invited Dherran Fitzgerald to live in his house. Sally Biegenwald was older, and it would be good to have someone younger there to help out with his mother if needed.

Biegenwald liked to do his "hunting" by the Jersey Shore, and often deposited the bodies in New York, mostly on Staten Island by his mother's house or the garage out back. Dherran Fitzgerald usually accompanied him. He liked Biegenwald's fearlessness. *"He was lazy, though,"* Dherran often complained when it came to body disposal and sometimes didn't remember where he buried them. Biegenwald killed for the thrill of the kill.

Biegenwald delighted in seeing the last lights of life fade from a victim's eyes. The glitter in their eyes fades and seems to coat over in a white or blue haze. Whatever expression the victims had during those last milliseconds of life was frozen on their faces. Sometimes, Biegenwald liked to strangle them, just to see their eyes pop out and their mouths open when they tried to suck in oxygen. They sometimes jerked up their necks, and one could see every nerve and sinew on their necks expand.

When they were shot, it went quick, but the look of the shock of pain on their faces was surreal. Biegenwald often wondered what it felt like to have a bullet tear through your innards.

October Surprise

Generally there weren't too many young women on the streets of Point Pleasant in the fall. The beach at Point Pleasant wouldn't be open until Spring, but one day in 1981, a girl by the name of Maria Ciaella, a pretty girl with long black hair was walking through her development on Village Way. She borrowed money from her father, saying she was going to meet up with some friends and would be back by midnight. It was a fairly safe area, so he wasn't concerned.

She apparently met up with her friends and they went to the stores or to one of their homes. No one knew for sure. After midnight, a cop drove by on Route 88 when Maria was, no doubt, on her way home, but she was alone at that point. The policeman was on an urgent call, but made it a point to stop by that area again to check on her.

Later, when the cop returned, Maria was gone. The police call he responded to was a moderately long one, so she should have been somewhere on Route 88 by then. The cop drove up Route 88, but Maria wasn't anywhere to be seen.

By that time she was in Biegenwald's car. He was so very charming and politely offered her a ride home. *"It isn't far,"* she said, but then he promised her some weed. She smiled and climbed in his car.

Instead of taking her home, he took her to an abandoned grassy area, slammed her body to the ground and with his .22-caliber gun put two bullets into her forehead. Her eyes flew back in her head, which violently lurched backward. Bits of brains and bone flew out the back of her head, and lodged into the soft, sandy soil. The brain chunks looked like oatmeal. Biegenwald looked at that with amazement. He had always wanted to watch someone die like that.

April Fool

It was April 5 1982, when young, athletic eighteen-year-old Deborah Osborne was jogging along Route 88 with a girlfriend in Toms River, New Jersey—a shore area coveted by beachgoers.

They were on their way to the Idle Hour Bar just a short distance away in Point Pleasant so they hitchhiked. They had just turned eighteen and could now legally drink.

Biegenwald spotted the girls, promised them some marijuana and offered the two a ride. Both were interested, so they hopped in his car.

They stayed at the bar for a bit and while her friend was in the ladies' room, Biegenwald offered to take Deborah to his apartment. *"It's not far from here,"* he said. Deborah thanked him but turned him down. She was going to wait for her girlfriend.

Biegenwald then asked her to walk him to his car. As soon as he neared his car, he snatched her, threw her in the back seat, and took off. He drove to his house, took her out to the back field, and leaped on her with his knife. She screamed, pushed his body up and rocked herself back and forth, struggling to get free. That made him very, very angry. So he stabbed and stabbed her. The medical examiner counted twenty-one puncture wounds.

Biegenwald shoved Deborah into his trunk and headed to his mother's on Staten Island but didn't visit her. He opened the basement by one of the external doors, and dragged the bloody corpse down the stairs. The basement had a dirt floor and made the job easier. He took out an axe and chopped up the corpse. Chunks of muscle and bone flew all over. There wasn't much left to the girl, so it wasn't too time-consuming to just lightly spread some dirt over her. Then he fled.

Disappearance at the Beach

It was now August of 1982. Anna Olesiewicz agreed to meet with a few friends at the beach on Friday, August 27th. They were going to rent a room and spend the weekend together in Ocean Township by the Jersey Shore. She attended Camden County College and was looking forward to a final weekend at the beach before returning to college.

When her father came home from work on Sunday, August 29th, she wasn't back yet as planned. He wasn't sure which of her girlfriends she went with, so he made a few phone calls. No one he called had made the plans with her. Usually Anna was very responsible, and he didn't have to follow up on her. It was a mystery. That evening and for a number of days following that, he walked down the boardwalk and along the beach, showing beachgoers a photo of her. No one recognized her.

Five months later, two children were playing in the back of Burger King, a fast food take out restaurant and they spotted squawking seagulls circling around an area at the edge of the parking lot. Curiously, the boys investigated and found Anna's partially decomposed body. There were four bullet holes in her head.

Murder of William Ward

Former prisoners have a curious way of meeting up outside prison, but Ward had actually escaped from prison. In September of 1982, Dherran and Biegenwald met up with William Ward at their home in Asbury Park to plan a caper. Ward was a video game operator who was also a drug dealer. During their meeting, they got into an argument. It turned violent and Biegenwald lost his temper. He shot Ward four times and carried his body to Neptune City, where he buried him.

Killing of Betsy Bacon

Biegenwald loved the shore. Late one night in November of 1982, Biegenwald was driving down Route 71 in Sea Girt and saw Betsy Bacon walking to a drug store. He politely offered her a ride and she accepted. Just a short distance down the road, Biegenwald pulled out his gun and shot her twice in the head. Just like that.

It was late, so he decided to make the body disposal easy this time. Biegenald pulled up to his own house in Asbury Park and put her in the garage for the time being. On the following day, he drove the body to Tinton Falls, a picturesque town with short waterfalls. He didn't realize he'd have such trouble burying Betsy, but Tinton Falls has a lot of sandstone and the ground is rather hard. Therefore, he could only bury her in a shallow grave amid some underbrush.

Arrest and Conviction

On January 22, 1983, the police had enough evidence to secure the prosecution of Richard Biegenwald. They surrounded his house, and lured him outside where they slapped the handcuffs on him. When they searched the house, they found his comrade, Dherran Fitzgerald. Fitzgerald was the weaker of the two and the investigators enticed him into turning state's evidence against Biegenwald.

Biegenwald was successfully convicted of killing five people. He was sentenced to death in 1983, but the sentence was overturned on an appeal that went all the way to the State Supreme Court.

Biegenwald died March 10, 2008, of respiratory failure and kidney failure.

IV

Corey Hamlet

The Grape Street Crips

T HE CITY OF NEWARK, ONCE CONTROLLED BY the Italian mob from the Genovese, Gambino, Luciano and Boiardo crime families, became the "turf" of the street gangs by 2010.

The "Grape Street Crips" of Los Angeles had an east coast subsidiary set up like a million dollar business enterprise. The biggest differences between the Crips and a large corporation was the fact that their products were illegal drugs and their business was racketeering, robbery, murder, and tax evasion.

They had their "by-laws," their management hierarchy, their employee "manuals," their computer networks, and their security staff. The Crips ruled the streets by fear.

Sidewalks were stained with blood, and sometimes even peppered with body parts. Assault rifle shells lay everywhere. People were terrified every time they went shopping and secretly wished they didn't have to eat. Their eyes were cast down, but when they looked up, their eyes darted from side to side and behind them... just in case someone would leap out with a rifle.

These weren't people with money; most were on welfare. Two men standing together against a wall were usually selling drugs. Many of their sons and daughters were addicted to drugs. There were no jobs. Entrepreneurs had all but abandoned the city, save a few brave souls who wanted to bring commerce back. Newark was dying.

Note: Some victims listed below were assigned numbers because the authorities feared there would be reprisals against their families. John Simmons—below—was the only one since identified.

The Murder of John Simmons, Victim #1

On July 15, 2010, John Leroy Simmons, the owner of *Clinton Jeanz* lay in a huge pool of his own blood on the corner of Clinton Avenue and Bergen Street. His brains were spread all over the pavement. Residents of the Clinton Arms and Oak Brook Square apartments over the store froze inside their apartments. Many children lived there, and their parents feared that perhaps some would be caught in the cross-fire between rival gangs. It happened over and over again.

The Crips were set up not unlike the mob from times past. The Genovese crime family engaged in racketeering. One of their favorite schemes was to intimidate legitimate store owners to "pay for protection," that is, to pay protection money to be "insured" against vandalism, theft, and other violent acts. That is extortion. The store owners were also expected to permit gang members to operate with impunity within these establishments, helping themselves to clothes or cash from the register.

John Simmons objected to making such payments. He was one of the first blacks who established their own businesses in Newark. Simmons was very proud of that. Because he, too, was black like most of the people in Newark, including members of the gangs, he felt that was a sign of racial disloyalty.

Simmons' body was left uncovered on the street, much to the horror of the people who lived there. The Councilman and future mayor, Ras Baraka, rushed to the scene when he heard that Simmons didn't even have the dignity of being brought to the morgue, and there was no forensic team present. Why? Because this was Newark, and nobody cared. That is, except those low-income people who wanted a better life for themselves and their families.

What was the motive for the shooting of Simmons? That was unknown, but no doubt was something to the effect that he failed to pay his "protection" money, or disrespected one of a member of the Crips. The killing was assigned by Corey Hamlet and his man, Tony Phillips, a.k.a. "Blue."

The N.J. Crips, like their Los Angeles brethren, were always recognized because they unabashedly wore a "uniform," of purple and blue bandannas, a logo, hat and clothing.

The Organizational Structure

1. The administrative members were ranked and their status was designated by letters including "OG" for "original

gangster" and classified downward to "BG" for "baby gangster." Besides those positions, there were overseers and enforcers. The overseers were in charge of certain geographic areas of the city. The enforcers were those who assaulted or killed offenders.

2. There was a disciplinary system including being stripped of one's rank, being put on probation, being physically assaulted or being killed.

3. Newark was divided into territories including: a) the 6th Avenue location near Irvington, b) the Pennington Court public housing complex, c) the Oscar Miles public housing complex, d) the Millard Terrell Homes, e) John W. Hyatt public housing complex, Georgia King Village public housing project, and f) the James Baxter public housing complex.

The gang was well-supplied with firearms and had an arsenal stored on the rooftop of a garage and in two other locations. The cache included numerous handguns, a .410-caliber assault rifle, a .45-Thompson semi-automatic carbine, a 7.62-caliber assault rifle, a 9mm Ruger P89 semi-automatic, a Calico M100 .22LR carbine, and a 9mm Cobray semi-automatic pistol.

Heroin was distributed in large bricks labeled either "Kiss my Ass," or "Spartacus." The cost was five thousand dollars each. Bricks consisted of five bundles of heroin. Each bundle contained a packet of five "hits" or "doses" of heroin.

Crack-cocaine was sold in clips. A clip was a package of crack-cocaine containing glassine envelopes with ten "hits" of crack and the words "Obama Care" on each one.

The Murders of Allen Best and Jarid Smith

On Christmas Eve, 2010, a few people were shopping near South 12th Street and Avon Avenue. They were picking up some last-minute items for their Christmas dinners. Mary Wiggins was one of those shoppers. She was in the liquor store when she heard the explosion of gunfire and ducked behind the cashier's counter.

It was four thirty in the afternoon, and *"People were closing up their stores. People were just scattering,"* Mary Wiggins told the city newspaper.

Right up the street, Allen Best and Jarid Smith were going to buy some boots with Best's Christmas money. Gunfire erupted again. Blood splashed all over the sidewalk and five victims, including Smith and Best, fell, screaming in pain. Witnesses were questioned, but were afraid of retribution by the Crips, so refused to release their names to the police, except for Willie Smith, Jarid's uncle. He had to identify the body of his nephew at the morgue.

The grandparents of Allen Best asked that police take them there to identify their grandson. They regretted ever giving him the money.

The ambulances squealed to the scene and rushed the victims to University Hospital, which was called Martland Medical in those days. That hospital housed the N.J. School of Medicine and Dentistry in partnership with Rutgers State University. Nearly every evening, the harried medics burst through the emergency room doors with gunshot and assault victims. Only the rough and hardened medical personnel could work there.

On the next day, the Newark Star Ledger said, *"No one has been arrested in the shooting."*

This area was a short distance from Market Street, the main North-South Street in Newark. Back in the day, there was a huge market at the base of the street which sold fish caught off of Port Newark. Fresh grapes were also sold there, which people used to make their own wine. Those days were over and gone, once the street gangs came in.

The Murder of Rodney Kearney

On the same night, December 24, 2010, Rodney Kearney sat inside a black SUV in a parking spot near the corner of Court and Broome Streets. Hamlet and Phillips flew by in their unidentified vehicle and shot him outright. He was raced to University Hospital and died there. Word on the street was the fact that Kearney was an innocent victim and the other young man was the intended target.

Just one month prior, on November 30, the mayor, Cory Booker, had laid off over one hundred police officers and that gave rise to a community uproar. The mayor indicated he'd had to make budget cuts.

Surveillance and Social Media

Hamlet used social media to contact his gang members, inform his gang of events, pass along information, and warn off potential enemies. Most of it was done publicly, but the police got legal permission to tap all the relevant telephone conversations of gang members.

Quite frequently Hamlet contacted his man, Kwasi Mack a.k.a. "Welches," who controlled the heroin and drug traffic in the

South 6th Avenue area in the neighboring towns of Orange and Irvington, New Jersey.

On May 30, 2012, Mack had been detained at the Essex County Correctional Facility. He called Hamlet to help in his defense by raising funds to hire an attorney. Mack then spread the word to his own man, Justin Carnegie, to secure some money from the drug profits, saying, *"Get that shit from 'Wax' (Eric Concepcion), grab that grand ($1000) from the nigga, um, 'Keem' (Hakeem Vanderhall)."*

While incarcerated, Mack a.k.a. "Welches," bragged to fellow inmates, *"I'm in the field. I'm beefin' with niggas. I'm at war. I'm a gangsta."*

Carnegie bragged from behind bars, *"Fuck the feds. They ain't stopping me. They trying to bury me all the time, the prosecutor has it out for me. I ain't sitting in the county (county detention center). I'm going to 'pop bail' (make bail). I'm going to go to trial. I'm a pick twelve (12 years). Fuck these crackers (whites). I ain't scared of no jail!"*

While Mack was in prison, Hamlet made arrangements to pick up the profits from the sales of drugs. During that time, he sent out

91

instructions to have two members of Mack's unit, Vanderhall and Concepcion, pick up the profits from the sale of crack-cocaine.

On that case, due to the work of a slick lawyer, Kwasi Mack was released the following year. Hamlet excitedly made the announcement on the street by posting on *Twitter.*

"The wait is over!!!!! #miniMe done touched down...#WELCHES #SHHHHH!!!!!"

By "#miniMe," Hamlet meant his #1 enforcer, Kwasi Mack, a.k.a. "Welches," and the rest of the message meant that Mack had been released from jail and was back on the streets. The charge is unknown, but most likely was for the illegal possession of a firearm.

The Murder of Victim #2

On May 3, 2013, Corey Batts and Tony Phillips shot Victim #2 in downtown Newark near Avon Avenue. His skull was shattered by multiple gunshots and blood and bone were propelled in many directions. The murder was done on orders from Hamlet. He indicated that Victim #2 was a close associate of Victim #1, who attempted to shoot Hamlet back in 2012, as an act of vengeance.

Corey Batts was ranked as "BG" in the organization, as he was only fourteen at the time of the murder.

As a warning to others who might be disloyal, Victim #2's body was left near Clinton Avenue. For a couple days, it rotted on the street, picked at by ravenous crows and surrounded by swarms of flies.

Attempted Murder of Victim #3

While Corey Batts, one of the gang members was incarcerated, he felt that the unidentified individual labeled "Victim #3" had something to do with his arrest and asked to have him assaulted. Although court records remain hidden as to the identity of Victim #3.

The Murder of Anwar West: Instagram Murder

Corey Hamlet hated rivals in his racketeering and drug trafficking business. Amalik Anderson was his major rival. Hamlet was an intelligent and clever man. Because he would be the most obvious suspect, Hamlet needed to set up a conspiracy to do away with Anderson and other rival gang members.

Hamlet also ordered the murder of Anwar West, whom he considered disloyal and charged Washington with that as well.

On October 7, 2013, fourteen shots rang out. West was shot dead in his Jeep Cherokee.

Attempted Murder of Amalik Anderson and Saidah Goines

Hamilton had a standing order for his gang to murder Amalik Anderson, his main rival. Ahman Manley and Tony Phillips took up the task. On October 27, 2013, they shot at a car being driven by Anderson. His girlfriend, Saidah Goines, was also in the car at the time. They were only wounded.

Hamlet also used the power of *Instagram* posts to spread the word among the criminal community that Anderson had "made a statement to the police." Hamlet kept up those posts, but the plot did not result in Anderson's death. A second attempt to murder Anderson only resulted in him being badly wounded by Hamlet's hit man, Rashan Washington, a.k.a. "Shoota,' on November 12, 2013, near the notorious street, Avon Avenue.

Attempted Murder of Victim #4

On October 27, 2013, Hamlet had Corey Batts, Ahmad Manley, and Tony Phillips attempt to kill Victim #4 when he was on the street. The victim wasn't fatally injured, but Batts was shot in his hand. Phillips brought him to St. Michael's Hospital. Batts was registered under a false name and when the police questioned him about the gunshot wound, he said very little.

Murder of Victim #5

On November 13, 2013, the unidentified Victim #5 was killed under the direct orders of Hamlet because it was suspected that he was a police informant and conspired with Victim #4 and Victim #1, to turn in some of the gang members. This murder occurred near Court Street.

The Murders of Wesley Child and Velma Cuttino

On March 3, 2014, Hamlet placed a hit on Maurice Green and participated in doing this himself along with Ahmad Manley. Green was the brother of Hamlet's nemesis, Amalik Anderson.

Hamlet and Manley set off a high-speed chase through the east-west avenues of Newark. Hamlet was in his Jeep Cherokee and

Green was in an Oldsmobile Alero along with a gang member of Anderson's crime ring, Wesley Child. The vehicles went racing down Irvine Turner Boulevard, but Green's vehicle crashed into several cars at the intersection of the Boulevard and Spruce Street. Green leaped out of his vehicle, and Hamlet shot a volley of bullets at him. Hamlet wounded Green but shot an innocent woman, Velma Cuttino, straight through her head. She was in another car at that fateful intersection.

Arrests

In May 2015, many of the members of the Grape Street Crips were arrested and charged with racketeering, murder, drug trafficking, firearms offenses, and attempted murder.

In November 2016, Corey Hamlet and more gang members were charged for twenty-two offenses including murder, acts of violence, drug trafficking, firearms offenses, witness intimidation, attempted murder, and racketeering.

As they were being held, along with Hamlet, the State of New Jersey was building a case.

"People think street gang members are not as smart as white-collar criminals. But Corey Hamlet is as smart as any CEO we've prosecuted," US Attorney Craig Carpenito said in his statement.

Sentencing

The Grape Avenue Crips were sentenced depending upon their pleas and the dates of their arrests. A portion of the gang was arrested in May of 2015, and the rest in November of 2016.

Sentences were passed on different dates depending on their pleas and the prosecutors' cases.

The Sentences:

Corey Hamlet—two concurrent terms of life imprisonment for murder, attempted murder, racketeering, assaults with a deadly weapon, distribution of illegal drugs, and firearms violations.

Hakeem Vanderhall—eighteen years for drug trafficking and racketeering.

Eric Conception—eighteen years for drug trafficking and racketeering.

Kwasi Mack—forty-five years for murder, racketeering, and the use of a deadly weapon.

Ahmad Manley—life imprisonment for murder with a ten year mandatory minimum, ten years for racketeering, and twenty years for assault with a lethal weapon.

Tony Phillips—mandatory life sentence on the murder and racketeering charges.

Justin Carnegie—twenty-five years for murder, racketeering, and drug distribution.

Corey Batts—six to twenty years for murder in New Jersey. However, Batts had killed before. In 2006, when he was a juvenile, he killed sixteen-year-old Clarence Edwards in the state of Pennsylvania, but wasn't apprehended until he was in New Jersey.

The Commonwealth of Pennsylvania sentenced Batts thirty years to life. All appeals on the basis of his being a juvenile were denied. His New Jersey sentence is being served concurrently with the sentencing in Pennsylvania, meaning he will be incarcerated for thirty years at least.

Rashan Washington—thirty years for murder, racketeering, use of illegal firearms, and the distribution of illegal drugs.

What's Left?

After the Genovese and the Gambino crime families wiped out much of the tax money in the city by taking it "off the books" through their drug sales and racketeering, they moved to Port Newark, where they continued their extortion and racketeering schemes.

Then people like Corey Hamlet and his Grape Street Crips came in. Like the crime families that preceded them, they continued to wipe out the tax base that a city should collect. Federal monies came in to help the financially struggling city, but some of it was lost to corrupt politicians and poor business and political management along the way.

Many, if not most, of the public housing units have been boarded up, as the former tenants have fled the city. They have migrated elsewhere, but their whereabouts is, as yet, unknown. Sections of Newark bear little resemblance to a city, as there are many empty lots cluttered with litter. Some new buildings being erected, and events being staged to attract the general public. However, when the entertainers leave, the streets empty and the discarded waste paper rolls like tumbleweed when the eerie silence of night descends.

Newark is a city that died due to the crime committed by the Crips and the other gangs, as well as the crime families that preceded them. For over twenty years, they caused a chronic loss of revenue.

Today, there are some signs of recovery, but it will take generations to heal. Such is the legacy of inner-city crime.

V

Robert Reldan

Ten Million Dollar Killer

The Pampered One

FORT LEE IS AN UPPER-MIDDLE-CLASS community and Robert Reldan was born there and into wealth. He was a gifted athlete and academically advanced. Unlike other young men his age, as an eighteen-year-old, he hob-knobbed with the jet-setters and trend-setters as well.

He loved flying to Europe first-class and loved scuba diving in the Caribbean. He had everything he could want because of the indulgence of his aunt, Lillian Booth, the widow of the owner of

IBM. But how can a young virile man find fun when he didn't have to work to make its reward worthwhile?

What thrill is there in having all you want?—Reldan liked hot cars. All he had to do was buy them. That was easy. There was no challenge in that. But—what if he *stole* cars? There was a sense of adventure with that. It would be fun, certainly. So, in 1958, he stole them. He was convicted, but his wealthy relatives saw to it that he didn't serve time in jail.

In 1963, his compulsion to try a new adventure overcame him again. Something he could do right out in the open would be bold and brazen. So, he stole lady's purses from them in elevators. Most of them screamed, and that made him laugh. He was charged, but his influential relatives came to the rescue. He served no time and made restitution. He was the pampered one.

Just Wait—The Killer Cometh!

He raped a woman in 1969, whose identity has not been released. That excited him immensely. But Reldon was personally greedy. It wasn't enough. He had to OWN the woman, he had to CONTROL her. However, he couldn't do it now. He had to struggle inside for just a little longer to have his real chance to be like a god with the control over everything and anything he wanted.

For that rape, Reldon wasn't excused from punishment. He was sentenced to five years and remanded to a rehabilitation facility intended to cure young men from a life of crime. The program was intended for those for whom the prognosis looked positive.

"Just wait though... you don't know my power yet."

Reldan was highly intelligent and manipulative, so he knew how to tell psychologists just what they wanted to hear. He fooled them and he fooled them thoroughly. In 1970, Robert Reldan was their first graduate.

A Second Chance

Reldan was then required to attend some out-patient sessions at the Rahway Sex Offender's Program. Religiously, he attended them. Very proudly, the country's most well-known talk show host, Robert Frost, interviewed Reldan. They raved about the success of the sex offender rehab program. Reldan smiled broadly. He knew he'd pulled it over on them.

In the Meantime

Mary Ann Pryor and her dear friend, Lorraine Kelly were "high school pretty." They loved shopping and there were sales at the Garden State Plaza mall in Paramus in 1974. It was perhaps a half-hour drive from Ridgefield, at the bus stop where Kelly's boyfriend, Ricky Molinari, dropped them off. However, a young man—good-looking and clean-shaven—picked them up. Normally they didn't hitchhike, but times were more innocent then, and the guy was really polite.

Reldan was a charmer. He didn't drop them off at the mall. He pulled over to a patch of bushes behind a motel. They screamed, but no one heard them. He tore their clothes off, and rolled them over. Reldan stomped his lit cigarette into their smooth bodies. They screamed harder, and he gagged both of them. This was going to be thrilling—two deep, warm vaginas for the taking.

Picking up a branch, he then whipped the girls and delighted in the bright red stripes that decorated their backs. Reldan was prepared. He had fashioned his own garrote—a thick rope tied on a strong stick, which he could turn and turn to tighten around their necks.

Reldan had been a sky diver and a pilot. He felt he could conquer the heavens. He could fool the psychologists with all their strings of degrees. He was smarter than them. It felt good.

He could control the minds of the most intelligent men they had. Now he realized he could control the bodies.

Susan Heynes

On October 6, 1975, Susan Heynes disappeared from her home in Haworth, New Jersey. Her husband called the Haworth Police Department, and a missing person's file was created. She was last seen by a neighbor in her front yard. The local newspaper, the Bergen Record, exploded with the news because the disappearance was so mysterious. One minute, she was in her front yard, and the next minute, she was missing. Her car was still parked at the house and this was the middle of the day.

Susan Reeve

On October 14, 1975, a driver was heading down Anderson Avenue in Demarest. He saw a bus stop and a lovely young teen disembarking. Coming home from school no doubt. Then the driver saw a car stop alongside her. Someone picked her up.

The girl had looked hesitant at first, but then got into a maroon station wagon. The driver wondered about that, but didn't stop. The man had to pick up his daughter at school, so he drove on. After collecting his daughter, he drove back along Anderson Avenue. The car he saw was gone. He then assumed—and hoped— all was well.

A toll worker on the Interstate heard some screams from the trunk of a maroon station wagon and called the police. The police showed the attendant mug shots, and she identified Robert Reldan.

Unaware he had been identified, Reldan took Susan to Talman State Park in Rockland County, New York. The park was on the highlands of the Palisades, not too far over the New Jersey border. It was a picturesque and yet isolated place.

Reldan grabbed Reeve, who was screaming and squirming. Like an animal, Reldan ripped off her clothing and raped her incessantly. He had his garrote handy and wrapped it around her neck. He tightened it, but not to the point she choked. The fight of death fascinated him, so he watched her cling to life. Then, finally, he gave the garrote its final twist. Her face tightened up in an unhuman grimace, the eyes rolled back, and turned white.

Flipping her over, he took his knife out and carved a large cross on her wrist. Then Reldan fled.

A person exploring the park at this chilly time of the year came across Reeve. He frantically called the police. The investigation was extremely thorough. A huge van called the Mobile Crime Scene Operations squealed to the scene and erected a huge white and yellow tent. They had nearly every piece of technical equipment that a forensic lab contained.

An army of investigators swarmed on the scene and picked up every fragment of organic matter that they could connect to the murder—samples of possible DNA from hair, clothing threads, swabs from her vagina, mouth, and even the ears. There were tissue papers strewn all over the body. Each was labeled and put in a plastic bag for analysis.

Police photographers were taking pictures of every single piece of evidence they saw. Detective Inspector Bales of the Metropolitan Police arrived with his men. They looked down at the woman and lapsed into total silence. Every part of her body had been beaten.

Bales leaned down. A tear glistened in his eye. The girl looked so innocent.

His partner, Detective Specialist Hughes then said, *"This is not an ordinary murder."*

"It looks like we have a serial killer," commented Bales. *"Call in that Reldan fellow."*

Reldan had been identified by the toll attendant.

Reldan Interrogation

On October 27, 1975, Reldan came in for questioning. They questioned him regarding Susan Heynes, and Susan Reeve as well. Reeve lived very close to Heynes, so they thought they'd ask about her too.

Reldan acted very conceited, and made it a point to indicate that his family had a lot of money. When asked about the days in question—October 6 and October 14—Reldan had alibis. The police questioned the sources, and they checked out.

Just to be sure they were drawing the right conclusions, the police asked that he take a polygraph test. Reldan said he wanted to hire a lawyer first and would return for the polygraph.

Reldan never returned.

Heynes' Body Discovered

On October 27, the Rockland Police received a call. Someone had found the body of Susan Heynes. She was discovered in the woods behind some homes in Valley Cottage, New York. That community was also in Rockland County and just thirteen miles away from Talman State Park where Susan Reeve's body was found. She had been brutally beaten and raped.

FBI Steps In

Because the bodies were of women who had disappeared from New Jersey and found in New York, the FBI became involved and worked closely with the New Jersey investigators. They all suspected Reldan, or another man by the name of Richard Cottingham. The FBI called in William Prendergast as a consultant. Prendergast was the head of the Rahway correctional program for sex offenders that Reldan attended. He was, of course, very disappointed that Reldan was implicated in the rapes and murders, and contributed what personal information he could to help apprehend him.

Break and Enter

One item Prendergast mentioned in his discussions with authorities was the fact that people with Reldan's personality profile like publicity about themselves, even bad publicity. According to Prendergast's prediction, Reldan broke into a home in Closter, New Jersey, an upper-income neighborhood.

When the owner of the house arrived home, he was startled by the presence of Reldan rifling through his wife's purse. As soon as that happened, Reldan fled in a 1969 red Opel. Wisely, the homeowner took close note of him.

Police then started surveillance of the neighborhood, and came upon a red Opel on the very same street. The registration belonged to Reldan, and the police were able to get a search warrant on the spot.

After the break and enter, police had enough evidence to arrest Reldan. They used the time during his incarceration on the break and enter charge to impound and examine his car. In the car, they found human hairs belonging to Susan Heynes and Susan Reeve. In addition, they found an engagement ring that was identified by the jeweler who originally sold it, as it was rather unique. He was charged with break and enter and robbery as well. He was sentenced to three years for that crime.

While serving his sentence for the robbery, Reldan was charged with the murders of Susan Heynes and Susan Reeve. Although the

District Attorney wanted to charge him for the murders of Lorraine Kelly and Mary Ann Pryor, they lacked sufficient substantial evidence to bring the case to court.

Reldan Wasn't Finished Yet

While in the Trenton State Prison awaiting his trial, Reldan made two mistakes. Those mistakes proved that he wasn't as intelligent as he pretended to be. Sometimes fear has the effect of stunting sound judgement.

First of all, Reldan told a fellow inmate that he killed the two girls, Mary Ann Pryor and Lorraine Kelly. He also admitted that his aunt, Lillian Booth, was rich, and he wanted to plot a way to grab his inheritance.

That gave the investigators the opportunity of setting up a "sting" operation. Posing as a hit man, a Bergen County detective contacted Reldan. They discussed this so-called murder, and the undercover officer recorded all their conversations.

Reldan was then charged and convicted of conspiracy for the plot to murder his aunt. Reldan was sentenced to a term of twenty to fifty years. His murder trial was pending.

111

Reldan Rebounds

A jury trial for the murders of Mary Ann Pryor and Susan Reeve was conducted in October 1975. However, the case was termed a mistrial because Reldan saw to it that five of the jurors were bribed. In addition, a technical error occurred when the court was mistakenly informed about the previous rape he had committed in 1969.

Once the matter with the aberrant jurors was taken care of, a new trial was convened later and held in 1986. Reldan became desperate, and in a wildly impulsive attempt to escape, Reldan leaped from the window of the third floor of the courtroom. They recaptured him and sent him to the prison hospital.

Once he was sufficiently recovered, the court was reconvened in 1986. In a wheelchair, with his feet badly swollen, he was retried and convicted of second-degree murder for the killing of Mary Ann Pryor and the first-degree murder of Lorraine Kelly.

He is currently imprisoned in the New Jersey State Prison.

Ten Million Dollar Settlement

On April 1, 2019, the family of one of Reldan's victims, Susan Reeve, won a huge settlement because of the death of their daughter. According to the family, the money is to be donated to a scholarship fund at her alma mater, Hollins University in Roanoke, Virginia.

VI

Richard Cottingham

The Torso Killer

RICHARD FRANCIS COTTINGHAM, AN UPPER-middle-class businessman, was an executive with Metropolitan Life Insurance Company in 1966. He lived in River Vale, New Jersey, with his parents.

River Vale was a classy community—full of families born into wealth, but also populated by the "wealth wannabees." The "wannabees" couldn't really afford the rich name-brand furniture or the interior decorators to distribute imitation ancient artifacts around their homes. The interior rooms of a "wannabee" home had very little furniture, although the front yards were meticulously landscaped. A "wannabee" house was like a stack of pretty boxes just for show, but empty inside. But who knew?

And who knew about the evil rolling around in Cottingham's head? These slithering mental demons eventually transforming him into a monster called "The New York Ripper," even though most of his murders occurred in New Jersey.

Cottingham was a commuter of opportunity. Soon afterward, he merited the name "Torso Killer." It tickled his fancy to imagine cutting... cutting the smooth-skin of a woman, and he was mesmerized leering at her blood as it oozed out. He liked to chew hair; he liked to lick; he liked to bite. But most of all, he relished chopping and dismembering bodies.

Sex, by its nature is aggressive but most "nice boys" do it gently and leave their lovers' bodies intact. Cottingham didn't. He preferred to treat his women like a butcher and test how intensely he could orgasm while breaking up their bodies. He didn't wear a butcher's apron though. He was a hot-shot business executive who wore a business suit.

Cottingham had a sharp mind, and became a computer software engineer while computer science was still in its infancy. That put him in good standing financially as he moved up the ladder. He worked for his father in that position at the Metropolitan Life Insurance Company.

By nature, most sons prefer to get out of the shadow of their parents and establish their own career as soon as they can. Cottingham wanted to be his own man. As soon as he could, he got a position with one of the largest and most prestigious companies in New York—Blue Cross and Blue Shield Association.

Despite the fact that work in the challenging new world seemed trendy and exotic, it was repetitious and boring. He made a lackluster salary, as he was starting at the bottom. Cottingham liked Manhattan, so he spent time there. There were sex workers in Times Square and on 9th Avenue and he liked gawking at them. Cottingham had big plans for them—very big plans. They were prostitutes selling their bodies, so Cottingham felt he had the right to their bodies.

However, he couldn't afford to live in Manhattan, but no longer wanted to live with his parents. So he moved to Little Ferry, New Jersey, and found a nice apartment complex, Ledgewood Terrace. The girls there was more delicate, so he figured he'd use them "just for practice."

First Murder

Nancy Vogel was his first trophy. One day in 1967, he ran into Nancy Shiavo Vogel at the Garden State Shopping Mall in Paramus, New Jersey. They knew each other from Little Ferry where she also lived.

Nancy and Cottingham carried on a cordial conversation when they met at the mall. She cut the conversation short, though, saying she was supposed to be at a Church Bingo affair and had to rush out.

He casually walked her to her car, but then that powerful urge overcame him and he leaped on her and threw her in the back seat of her car. She screamed frantically. He sucked in a feeling of power from that. Then he tore off all her clothes. What cute panties she had on! And a cuter ass underneath. It made him salivate and his penis grew hard and dripped.

He grabbed her hands and tied them together. It looked like she was in a fetal position. He had perfect control now.

He drove to Montvale. There was a small park there with overgrown grass, so he dragged her out of the car. He sodomized her until she bled, flipped her over and raped her until he was exhausted. With a rope, he strangled her.

Cottingham derived pleasure from hearing Nancy gag on her own saliva. She nearly swallowed her tongue in an effort to breathe. Once she was listless, he drove her car to a parking lot in Ridgefield Park nearby. There he could catch a local bus and go home.

Vogel's murder was lackluster, he thought, so he tried to develop ideas as to how to make the killings more thrilling.

Trophy Two

Cottingham liked Bergen County. There were a lot of attractive homes there, filled with beautiful women and girls. This was almost more fun than cruising around Manhattan. He could walk around the picturesque neighborhoods landscaped with bushes and azaleas that bloomed so nicely in the summer.

On July 17, 1968, he spotted sweet young thirteen-year-old girl, Jacalyn Harp, walking home in Midland Park. She'd obviously been at band practice because she had a leather sling around her used to hold a band flag. He pulled up to her and offered her a ride. He knew he looked like the proper gentleman all dressed up in his black suit. It was the perfect cover for perversion.

118

Jacalyn had been well-trained by her parents and teachers not to accept rides from strangers, so she politely refused. Cottingham looked her up and down. His earlier victim, Nancy, had been twenty-nine. *Wouldn't it be great enjoying a young child?*

He followed her slowly in his car. Young Jacalyn became alarmed and walked even faster. Cottingham became impatient. He overtook her, pulled over, and dragged her into his car. He spotted a wooded area—the teens called the "Washies"—where they used to hang out and smoke. He forced her over there. She was a real "wiggler!"

He threw her on the ground, ripped off her clothes, gagged her and tied her up. Then he had his way with her. The girl bled from her vagina as he thrust into her over and over. It was a snug fit. She moaned loudly, so he squeezed her tender neck with the leather strap used for carrying the band's flag. Then he cut off her arms and breasts and left her there. Jacalyn Harp was found the very next day.

The Hackensack Beauty

In April 1969, Hackensack was an ideal place for shopping. Attractive dress and shoe shops along Ridgewood Avenue. Bell-bottom or slim jeans with silver belts, nicely knitted sweaters, and high heels adorned the store windows. Eighteen-year-old Irene Blasé, took a bus there from her home town in Bogota. Those stores had the trendiest clothes that would be a hit with the boys at school.

Cottingham liked to walk the streets in those shopping areas, because he could shop for girls. He spotted Irene Blase. Although she was a senior in high school, Cottingham felt she was still "high school pretty." Cottingham walked beside her for a while, and started up a friendly conversation. After she went into a few stores, he suggested they have a drink. *"You're old enough, now,"* he remarked.

He told her he knew of a nice quiet place just a short distance away, so they took the local bus there. After sitting with her for a while chatting, he said he had his car parked in the city parking lot, but could drive her back to her bus station if she liked. Irene agreed and climbed in his vehicle.

Cottingham didn't drive Irene to the bus stop, though. He drove her to Saddle River, an upper-crust town named after the river that wound through there. When he didn't go in the right direction, she screamed, but he had the windows shut until he could gag her. He pulled into the park alongside the river, tore off her clothes, cut her skin and nipples and caressed her body. He didn't rape her. He strangled her with either a cord or the chain from the crucifix she was wearing. That was the part he liked the best. Afterward, he rolled her right into the river.

Passersby saw Irene Blase's cut, bruised body in four feet of water.

Long-Haired Brunette

Cottingham preferred his girls with long hair. They seemed much sexier and alluring. On July 14, 1969, in Closter, New Jersey, he saw his next victim, Denise Falasca, fifteen years old. She was supposed to meet a friend, according to her parents, but never came home.

She was wearing the favorite trendy tight jeans of the day. They were bright pink and he liked her wiggle when she walked. Cottingham used his usual formula to attract her, that is, by offering her a ride. Oh, yes, she would be very happy for a ride, as her friend lived nearly a mile away. She climbed in his car and he drove in the wrong direction—toward Saddle Brook, and she protested.

They always did, it seemed. Cottingham noticed a golden crucifix hanging around her pretty neck and smirked. He had no use for religion. As long as she was the religious sort, he pulled over to a church in Saddle Brook and drove around to the cemetery behind it. All those tombstones stood like silent stony sentinels, and seemed not to care what he was doing. *Why use a nasty ole rope? How about the girl's crucifix?*

He gagged Denise and took off her blouse. What a surprise! A dainty pink bra to match her pink pants! Cottingham raped her repeatedly, took out his knife and cut into her body. Blood dripped out and ran down the smooth curves of her body. He tied her feet to her hands.

He wound up the necklace with the crucifix on it and twisted it around her neck until she bled. She gagged and her body humped up so she might be able to catch her breath. Cottingham pulled the chain tighter until it buried itself deeply into the skin on her neck. Then her eyes turned upward in her head and hazed over. Once she stopped moving, he dragged her over to edge of the cemetery as the spirits of the dead watched over her helplessly.

Wedding

Cottingham was a charmer. In 1970, he met a woman named Janet. Janet moved into the Ledgewood Terrace apartments with Cottingham. He was always very gentle with his wife when they engaged in sex, but it did arouse him to develop new techniques to make his attacks more sadistic.

Cottingham had been raised by rich parents and liked nice things. So, one day in 1972, he thought he'd get his wife a nice piece of jewelry. Cottingham, however, was adept at pilfering, so he was caught robbing from the jewelry counter at Stern's, in his favorite shopping center, the Garden State Mall in Paramus. He was convicted, but was let go with a fifty dollar fine. His wife was very humiliated by that and begged him not to embarrass her further.

In 1973, they gave birth to baby boy named Blair. The Ledgewood apartment would suit for a while, but Janet became pregnant again. As they wanted a nice neighborhood for their budding family, they rented a larger place—a three bedroom house on Vreeland Street in Lodi, New Jersey. On March 28, 1975, Scott, their second son was born.

Cottingham really didn't want the extra expense of the larger apartment, though, because he had a girlfriend on the side, Barbara Lucas. Unbeknownst to his wife, Cottingham often went over to Times Square after work to watch the street walkers.

Barbara Lucas was a prostitute from Manhattan who Cottingham had a particular fondness. She was in a lot of trouble with her pimp, and Cottingham felt sorry for her. He became her hero when he rescued her from her pimp. Cottingham then rented a room at the Quality Inn in Hasbrouck Heights, New Jersey, where she could stay and see him from time to time.

The Nurse

In 1977, Cottingham came across an X-ray technician by the name of Maryanne Carr. Cottingham knew her from the Ledgewood Terrace apartments where he once lived. She was a commuter who worked at a hospital in Englewood. Cottingham easily enticed her with a ride and took her to the Quality Inn in Hasbrouck Heights, New Jersey. He didn't rape her, but—for some unknown reason—cut off the leg of her white pants. He stripped her waist up, handcuffed her, cut her breasts and her chest then slashed his knife into her legs. Cottingham was very fond of bondage. He took out his trusty garrote and strangled her. It was thrilling watching a woman's last gasps.

He dragged her to the edge of the parking lot, and shoved her body against a chain-link fence.

New Torso Sensations!

In January of 1979, a hooker by the name of Helen Sikes went missing from her usual rounds near Times Square. All the way out in Queens, the police found her body with the head nearly hacked off. There were no legs on the body. After searching the area, the police found her legs a block away, Blood had collected all over the sidewalk.

Sometimes Cottingham came home early from work. He mused about developing new methods of attaining even greater sexual pleasure and more orgasms. His mind then floated back to those hardy street walkers in Times Square. He couldn't always get away to go to New York, but on December 2, 1979, he gave birth to a new and more advanced idea. There was an old hotel in Times Square, the Travel Inn Motor Hotel which he'd seen many times. It would be a good place to lure one of those prostitutes inside.

On the street, he spotted twenty-two-year-old Deedeh Goodarzi, an immigrant from Kuwait with a friend, whose identity is unknown. Those Arab girls had the silkiest darker hair he'd ever seen on women, so he offered to take them upstairs to a room. A nice double-duty trick.

Then he threw them on the bed and abused them to his heart's content. They screamed, so he had to gag them. He then raped, sodomized, and strangled them. Next, he pulled out his axe, the "piece de resistance." With a hideously evil smile, he chopped off their hands and heads. After shoving the body parts in the hotel laundry bag, he splashed them with lighter fluid, took out his cigarette lighter and set them on fire. As expected, the fire alarm blared and he fled the building.

What a thrill that was! He orgasmed just reflecting on it.

Divorce Attempt

In 1979, Cottingham's wife, Janet filed for divorce. He was hardly ever home, and she suspected him of having an affair. His mistress, Barbara Lucas, and he had a falling out when Cottingham met a new woman, Jean Connelly. He liked Jean a lot; she was steady and reliable, so he leaned on her for moral support.

In 1980, Janet Cottingham dropped the divorce she filed against him—for unknown reasons. She then moved to Poughkeepsie, New York, with their children.

The Cocktail Waitress

In 1980, Cottingham also met a dark-haired woman after he got out of work in Manhattan. She was a delectable cocktail waitress at Tuesday's restaurant he frequented. Her name was Karen Schilt. He took her home in his Maroon T-Bird and brought her to a wooded area behind his former residence in Little Ferry. He handcuffed her, then sodomized her, and raped her but didn't strangle her. He left her abused body up against a storm drain. She was unconscious, but later discovered and treated.

A month later, he was hot for a new victim and met a prostitute, Susan Geiger. He drove her to New Jersey and found a small motel in South Hackensack. Susan was pregnant, but he raped her anyways, then he beat her, knifed her, and left her for dead. She managed to get some help, and was brought to the Hackensack Hospital.

May 1980

Cottingham moved his base of operations from New York back to New Jersey. Why not pick up these "pretties" from among the prostitutes near Times Square and bring them closer to home?

He was then able to establish a "home away from home," and still have a chance to go home to see his children.

On May 5, 1980, Cottingham was prowling the prostitute district near Times Square and picked up Valerie Streets. She was lovely, with the long black hair he really liked. He drove her to New Jersey and rented a room at the Quality Inn Motel in Hasbrouck Heights, which wasn't too far from where he lived. He gagged her, handcuffed her feet and hands together, beat her unmercifully, then sodomized her and raped her. He cut her with his knife and strangled her.

Now, what to do about the body? Cottingham stuffed her under the mattress. The maid found the horribly disfigured corpse when she went in to clean the room.

On May 12, 1980, Cottingham was driving through Teaneck, New Jersey. In one of the community parking lots, he spotted a woman by the name of Pamela Weisenfeld. Unable to resist his deviant urges, he went after her and dragged her to a more secluded area near the lot. He offered her drugs, then without warning he beat her and bit into her breasts.

Fortunately, Pamela survived.

Cottingham worked on perfecting his mutilation procedure. He met one of the prostitutes that worked the area May 15, 1980, Mary Ann Reyner, and rented a room. After he molested her, he bit her nipples, knifed her in the chest, and sliced off her breasts.

Cottingham liked to see bright red blood flow. Then he took out his trusty garrote and strangled her. That always made him orgasm a second time. He squirted lighter fluid on her body and set it on fire.

While surveying the prostitute districts in Manhattan, he met up with Leslie O'Dell. Like Valerie, he took her to the motel in Hasbrouck Heights. Cottingham couldn't barely contain himself and leaped on her once they got to the room. He gagged her, beat her, and raped her incessantly. He then pulled out his garrote to finish her off.

Luckily, Leslie was able to holler for help. Neighbors heard her shrieks and called the police. Once he heard the squeal of the police sirens, Cottingham became frantic; rushed out of the motel but was arrested in the parking lot. It was now May 22, 1980.

Multitude of Charges and Trials

Cottingham's salaciously murderous rampage finally caught up to him. In August 1980, he was charged in New York for the homicides of Mary Ann Reyner, Deedeh Goodarzi, and "Jane Doe," the unidentified woman he picked up with Goodarzi.

In Bergen County, New Jersey, the grand jury delivered a twenty-one count indictment against him in September 1980. His first trial was held on June 6, 1981.

There is an old adage that states: "Anyone who represents themselves has a fool for a client." Cottingham, a man drowning in his own conceit, decided to represent himself. At the trial, he did admit that he was fascinated with bondage as a young child. Psychologically, he employed the defense strategy of massive denial, and made the outrageous claim that he had no intention whatsoever of hurting anyone! Four of his victims—Pamela Weisenfeld, Leslie O'Dell, Karen Schlit, and Susan Geiger—survived Cottingham's assault and testified against him. He had left a thumbprint on the handcuffs he used for the Karen Schlit murder.

The prosecution team, jumped on that horrendous confabulation of the facts. Forensic evidence was presented, and there was a great deal of it. In June of 1981, Cottingham was convicted of twenty of the twenty-one counts of first-degree murder against him, and incarcerated at the New Jersey State Prison. He was sentenced to one hundred seventy-three to one hundred ninety-seven years.

The trial for the murder of Mary Ann Carr was scheduled for a later date.

A Coward at Heart

Four days after hearing his sentence, Cottingham obtained some transmission fluid from the prison's auto workshop and drank it, hoping to die rather than face prison. They treated him, and he was then sent back to his cell.

Mary Ann Carr's trial was scheduled for February of 1982. However, Cottingham was so overcome with anxiety that he collapsed on his way to the court house, having developed a duodenal ulcer. A mistrial was declared until he could recovery sufficiently.

The new trial on the case of Mary Ann Carr was scheduled for October 4, 1982. Desperate and crazed by his own fear, Cottingham attempted to escape, but was thwarted in that attempt.

He was sentenced to twenty-five years to life for second-degree murder, with the term to run consecutively with his prior sentence.

There still remained the pending trial in New York for the murders of Deedeh Goodarzi, Mary Ann Reyner, and "Jane Doe." Cottingham was transferred temporarily to the Manhattan House of Detention to await that trial scheduled for July 9, 1984.

There, right in the courtroom, a desperate and depressed Cottingham pulled out a razor he had hidden in his suit and slashed his left wrist. He was treated for that self-injury and brought back into court to hear the sentence, which was seventy-five years to life.

He was then remanded to the New Jersey State Prison to serve his time. Among all the sentences he received since the 1967 murder of Nancy Vogel to the twenty-one count conviction in 1981, earned him a life term. At New Jersey State Prison.

VII

Khalil Wheeler-Weaver

Caught by a Dead Woman

ORANGE, NEW JERSEY, WAS ONE OF THOSE towns that survived the civil rights riots of the 1960s. The most noticeable change was the color change—from white to black. No problem with that—black Americans were getting the jobs once held by white Americans. Little by little, blacks were elected to office in Orange, East Orange, Irvington, and Newark.

The families were becoming middle-class Americans with the rights and privileges thereof. School systems were improving but in a limited way. Khalil Wheeler-Weaver had all the advantages of Federal Monies going into education.

Wheeler-Weaver graduated and obtained a job as a security guard. His family was proud of him, as he was taking early steps into the field of his father and stepfather.

Frustrated Sexual Urges

Because Wheeler-Weaver didn't fit the pattern of the other "cool" kids on the streets, he was forced to seek out avenues to satisfy his sexual desires. He knew that drugs were easy to obtain on the street, so he picked up some date-rape drugs and drove to Nye Avenue, in Newark, where the prostitutes hung out.

Worship of the Trends

You weren't "cool" if you weren't wearing designer jeans, or bouncing down the sidewalk in white Jordan's—the sneakers that said you were okay with the girls. Wheeler-Weaver didn't fit the lifestyle defined by the popular kids at East Orange High School. He wore plaid shirts.

He was accepted into Rutgers University in Newark, in the respected field of computer science. Regardless, some really liked him for his humor and appeal despite the "turn-off" behaviors. Because he wasn't into the "in" crowd, he couldn't attract women. Then the underclass of criminals piped sexual workers into downtown Newark, Orange, Irvington, East Orange and then into Montclair, where the Montclair College—which later became Montclair State University—was established.

Wheeler-Weaver's father was a retired police detective in the city of Newark—and tried to prevent the criminal elements that still remained. Black people were rising in social status. Wheeler-Weaver's stepfather was a policeman in the nearby town of East Orange. Both men were tough, but it was difficult raising a young man in an environment that still had the vestiges of organized crime.

The structure of government was designed by the likes of the Genovese crime family, molded by the white mayor, Hugh Addonizio. In 1981, Addonizio was arrested for corruption and thrown in jail. After all the political damage had been done, it was now up to the black people to correct a broken government, but without a healthy model to build upon.

Kenneth Gibson, Newark's first black mayor, was elected in 1970 and served until 1986. All the neighboring towns like Orange and Irvington followed the example set by Newark. Although Mayor Gibson tried, he walked into an economic base that had been robbed by the mobs. Making positive significant differences would take money... money that wasn't there. Large corporations were leaving the city and its tax base was diminishing.

The Genovese, Boiardo, and other crime families, were still subtly active behind the scenes, though. They spent their nights pumping narcotics into the young people of those towns, rendering the next generations virtually ineffective.

Because of narcotics, the underworld of crime still had some influence even under the administration of the Newark mayor, Res Baraka who was elected in 2014. There was some improvement, but it was incomplete. Streets of Newark and Orange consisted of nice middle class homes, but it was interrupted by abandoned houses and empty lots strewn with litter. There was evidence everywhere that the criminal blight had made its mark.

Initially, Wheeler-Weaver aspired to become a police officer like his stepfather. Before graduating, he got a job as a security guard at Sterling Securities, a firm founded by two Newark police officers. He was assigned to guard the Shoprite supermarket in Union, New Jersey, which was close by.

There Were Snakes

Snakes were rolling around in Wheeler-Weaver's head. Unknown to his family, Wheeler-Weaver wasn't patient. He wanted more. His parents both worked and couldn't keep him away from the negative environment of the streets that were still populated by drug-addled teens. The belief that "Might was Right" was the philosophy of the city. He had low impulse control over his sexual urges and little interest in fostering a healthy relationship with a woman.

Instead, he focused on keeping up with trendy clothes, popular music, and the externals that attracted the interest of women.

Killing of Robin West

Wheeler-Weaver was lucky enough to get his family to co-sign for a loan on a smart silver BMW, so he cruised Nye Avenue in Newark. It was a street frequented by prostitutes. On September 1, 2016, Breneisha Patterson and her girlfriend, Robin West, were walking down the street looking for a "john," that is, a man who would pay to have sex with them. They needed the money at that point because it was Robin's 20th birthday and they were broke. So, they decided to turn a trick.

Wheeler-Weaver saw them and pulled over in his sharp-looking BMW.

"Who do you want?" asked Breneisha Patterson.

Wheeler-Weaver pointed to Robin West, and she hopped in. He was quite charming, clean-cut, and nice looking. Smart, too. He had graduated from Rutgers University in Newark with a degree in computer science.

Wheeler-Weaver knew the towns quite well, and drove Robin to an abandoned house in Orange. She sensed she was in trouble when he seemed overcome with his sexual urges and treated her roughly. She screamed but he dragged her upstairs and raped her. Robin was a feisty gal and fought him off valiantly, but to no avail.

Wheeler-Weaver set out with murder in mind. It gave him a perverse thrill to finish his encounters with a sense of full and utter control over a woman. Therefore, he prepared well. He always brought his black leather gloves with him, as well as rope, and other supplies for the kill.

He orgasmed when he had sex and orgasmed again when he killed. After the rape, Wheeler-Weaver grasped Robin around the throat and strangled her. He loved to watch his victims struggle for oxygen. It made him feel like a god. Once her body went limp, he sprinkled it with lighter fluid and set it on fire. He fled on foot.

The raging fire spread through the multi-family building, which was mostly built of wood. Firefighters from the three towns around rushed to the scene. When the smoke cleared, the arson squad checked it out. They concluded it was deliberately set.

Then They Found Her

After checking the burnt remains of the building, the investigators discovered a body. The skin had been burnt to a crisp, and parts of the body had melded together. The discovery was a brutal one. After the forensic team analyzed the remains, they were able to identify Robin West by her dental records two weeks later.

Robin's parents, Anita Mason and Leroy West were frantic when they heard the tragic news. They'd been texting people who knew Robin, and then they heard from the authorities. The parents were also horrified to read in the Philadelphia newspapers headlines which included terms like "Philadelphia escort" and "Teenage Philadelphia Hooker." That wasn't their Robin, they said. She wasn't a prostitute—just a girl who occasionally had a fling.

Killing of Joanne Brown

The city of Orange, Wheeler-Weaver's favorite haunt, had magnificent homes that fell into disrepair when the town went spiraling down due to the rise of violence. Gorgeous Georgian mansions were converted into rooming houses, and were poorly kept up. Renters had to keep their food in communal refrigerators and their food was constantly being stolen.

As soon as the economy weakened, slum lords took advantage of those with limited incomes, and matters worsened. When people could no longer afford the rents, they left. Many returned to their families in other states. Then the abandoned Orange homes filled up with squatters.

The squatters were often drug addicts. They camped in the hallways and apartments. As there were no working toilets, buildings became filthy. In October of 2016, an older black man by the name of Jefferson Turner drove down one of the streets in front of a two-story abandoned home, which had magnificent pillars outside, and rot within.

He heard some screaming from the building. The man then called the police. When they investigated, the police found the strangled body of Joanne Brown, a student at Montclair State University.

When they questioned the neighbors, police obtained a description of the silver BMW Wheeler-Weaver had been driving. Someone on the block added that they saw a woman meeting Joanne Brown's description getting into the BMW.

Tagged

In order to assure himself of a steady stream of victims, Wheeler-Weaver decided to use his computer skills to attract them. Hence, he could determine the location of potential victims and lure them to meet him. He made use of the social media application *Tagged* to meet his victims.

The Potential Victim

On November 15, 2016, a victim who is currently referred to as "T.T." had a close encounter with this mad New Jersey killer. "T.T." was pregnant and without family support or friends to help her, so she was homeless.

To try to help herself, she contacted Wheeler-Weaver online. He readily agreed to meet with her for sex, and told her he'd bring her to a motel in Elizabeth. She then went to Elizabeth to meet him. Once she got in his car, he donned a ski mask.

It frightened her when he appeared in the mask and she screamed. He rushed at her in the back seat with duct tape and slapped it across her mouth and used it to tie her hands as well. Wheeler-Weaver was always aroused by bondage. He then raped her in the back of his BMW, and tried to strangle her, as he did with the other women.

"T.T." passed out as result of the strangulation. However, she did reach consciousness again, and begged him to take her to the motel as he promised. Perhaps believing that he'd get a chance for a second round with her, he did so.

No sooner did they get into the room, "T.T." locked the door and called the police.

Astonished at his naivete, Wheeler-Weaver then fled.

Killing of Sarah Butler

After his experience with "T.T.," one might think that Wheeler-Weaver would be more cautious. However, his sexual urges overcame his common sense. He felt he was untouchable and immune to prosecution. After all, his stepfather was a cop who could shield him if he was caught. Or so he thought.

Sarah Butler was a second-year student at the Jersey City University. She met Wheeler-Weaver online on *Tagged*. They had communicated from time to time, and Sarah entertained the idea of meeting him in person. When Sarah was out of college for her Thanksgiving holiday, she and Wheeler-Weaver touched base online. Wheeler-Weaver propositioned her for a sexual rendezvous and said he was willing to pay her five hundred dollars for the meeting.

Although Sarah wasn't a sex worker, that kind of money drew her interest. She jokingly texted him and asked, *"You're not a serial killer, right?"*

Naturally he denied that and she agreed to meet him. Sarah's mother permitted her to use the family van on November 22, 2016, "to meet a friend." No one ever saw her alive after that.

Eagle Rock Reservation

In South Orange, New Jersey, there is a beautiful nature preserve for the residents of the surrounding heavily suburban towns to explore. It is peppered with large rocks, nature trails, beautiful foliage, and picnic areas. There was even a pond hidden off the beaten path full of otters who frolic and play, and leap on and off the rocks.

At the nature preserve meant for pleasure and relaxation, Sarah Butler's body was found. It was disrespectfully buried under a pile of rotten leaves. She had been strangled, and her beautiful face was twisted into a morbid grimace.

The Late Sarah Butler's Friends Caught Him!

Butler's sister knew Sarah's passwords and logged into her *Tagged* account. Wheeler-Weaver's posts were there. Her parents investigated further and notified the police. They wanted justice for their dear daughter and all those innocents who had been caught up in Wheeler-Weaver's spider web.

They created a fake profile on *Tagged* and posted it, trying to coax a response from Wheeler-Weaver. The ruse worked! He agreed to a meeting with the imaginary woman in Montclair. On December 4, 2019, he arrived and the police arrested him.

Although Wheeler-Weaver was quite skilled at trying to cover his tracks online, police computer experts were smarter. They found his telephone records, with phone numbers traced back to Joanne

144

Brown, one of his victims. They also discovered that Wheeler-Weaver had been living at the abandoned house in Orange which he burnt down after killing Robin West. Evidence also suggested that this heartless serial killer watched the firemen put out the flames. Investigators were able to discover that he was not only looking for victims, but also for do-it-yourself poisons he could use.

Arrest

On December 4, 2019, Khalil Wheeler-Weaver was arrested. The trial was heard in December 2019. During the two month long trial, the damning evidence was presented, including his phone records, online contacts, forensic evidence, and testimony by witnesses who had seen him in his car with the victims. Wheeler-Weaver didn't take the stand.

He was convicted of the murders of three women plus the attempted murder of a fourth and the desecration of human remains. Wheeler-Weaver faces life plus eighty years in prison.

VIII

Robert Zarinsky

Caught by a Missing Woman

INDEN, NEW JERSEY, WAS A STEP REMOVED FROM a typical middle-class suburban community. Linden had a collection of ugly oil tanks for fuel storage. Anyone driving on the highways who spotted them said, *"Oh, we're in Linden."* The derivation of the word "Linden" came from the word "lime tree." Lime symbolizes love, friendship, and healing. The city didn't look as picturesque as the name implied. It was a name lost in history and now marred by the bastions of industrial society.

For Robert Zarinsky's victims, "Linden" was a term empty of meaning.

Officer Charles Bernoski

Charles Bernoski was a policeman in Rahway, New Jersey. On November 28, 1958, he spotted two men at Miller Pontiac breaking into the back building. Bernoski leaped out of his car and ran toward them. One man was Robert Zarinsky and the other—his cousin, Ted Schiffer. Schiffer needed some antifreeze and Zarinsky suggested stealing it. Zarinsky was a veteran robber, an arsonist, and often committed assault. Schiffer was just like Zarinsky, but not as well known by the police.

Officer Bernoski confronted them one by one and met with armed resistance. In the scuffle, he shot both of them, but Bernoski himself was shot and killed. The two injured boys rushed to Mrs. Zarinsky for help. Instead of taking them to the emergency room, she treated them herself. Once she heard that a cop was shot, she swore them to secrecy.

Zarinsky and Schiffer were both known to the cops, so they approached the house to interrogate them. Neither Zarinsky nor Schiffer were there at the time, so they spoke to Zarinsky's sister, Judith. She told them that her brother shot the cop. Only one fingerprint was found at the scene, but there was no match on file for it. The mystery went unresolved for nearly forty years. The police didn't know about Schiffer because he had no police record.

Mary Klinsky

Mary lived with her adult brother, as both her parents had died. They lived in the family house in Hazlet, not too far from the Keansburg town line. In the summer, people would drive down Route 36 into Keansburg to enjoy the long boardwalk and pleasant beach. Many people liked to walk the boardwalk for exercise and stop at the small shops alongside it.

Mary was a senior at Raritan Township High School and worked as a school library aide. She was well-liked and looked forward to graduation. Mary had a boyfriend who was in the Navy and out at sea. She planned on marrying him upon his return.

She and her family were of a lower income bracket, and worked hard to pay taxes and maintain their shore home there. Mary had signed up with some beauty schools, and knew she could make a decent living doing that.

On September 15, 1965, Mary strolled up to the deserted boardwalk to mail a letter to her lover at sea. Then she sat down on a bench to enjoy the ocean breeze. It was the end of the season and this was a chance to enjoy the memories of the past summer.

Then, suddenly, Zarinsky arrived. He was attracted to her beautiful blue eyes and long auburn hair. Would she like to take a walk? No, she indicated; she had to go home.

Suddenly, he grabbed her and dragged her down to a sandy patch under the boardwalk. She protested, but he covered her mouth with his hand. His car was right nearby in the parking area just behind the beach. He dragged her to his car, threw her in the back seat, and stripped her nude and ferociously raped her. She screamed, but there was no one near enough to hear. Then he beat her on her head until she lapsed into unconsciousness, her face frozen in an expression of fear.

He pulled on to the highway, and turned up a little-traveled road to Telegraph Hill in nearby Holmdel. There was plenty of grass and weeds and he tossed her out of the car and rolled her behind a bush. Then Zarinsky took off.

On the following day, her body was discovered by a maintenance worker. Investigators examined Mary and determined her skull was fractured and she bled internally into her brain.

They took her body to the county morgue. An investigation was initiated, but no suspect was targeted at that time.

Jane Durrua

East Keansburg was one of those New Jersey shore towns in which nature had preserved its original charm. There was one area devoted to an amusement park in its sister-town of Keansburg, but in its back areas, East Keansburg had its rough and wild saltmarshes. The seagrass grows prolifically behind the bungalows and small houses in the sandy soil.

On November 4, 1968, thirteen-year-old Jane Durrua was taking the shortcut home through the meadow and across the railroad tracks to her home. She was on her way from school. Zarinsky was there too.

Jane was lovely. Zarinsky desperately wanted to touch her. He became aroused and ran up to her and threw her to the ground. She was only wearing a small jacket and a skimpy dress, so he pushed it up, yanked off her panties and shoved his erect penis into her body. That hurt her and she cried out. The area was deserted, so no one heard. He pommeled her body over and over until he was sated.

Afterward, he choked her and pitched Jane's fragile body into one of the drainage ditches that crisscrossed the field. Then he left as abruptly as he came.

Her brother-in-law, Ronald Connors, went looking for her when she didn't come home. He followed a trail of her belongings—the little girl's purse, a sewing kit she had brought to school, and her school books. He eventually stumbled upon her body. Her skull had an enormous bump on it from having been hit with a blunt instrument.

The forensic team found semen on her slip, and traced it to Jerry Bellamy, a sex offender who was being detained at the Adult Diagnostic Center at the East Jersey Prison in Rahway. However, DNA science was still in its infancy.

In 2005, the Monmouth County prosecutor, Luis Valentin, had the evidence re-analyzed in the light of the more advanced medical technology. He discovered that there was a match to Robert Zarinsky, not Jerry Bellamy.

Valentin was in charge of investigating older cases of homicide in the shore towns, and looked into possible links to Zarinsky. He was drawn to the case of Jane Durrua when he noted that the originally accused offender was Jerry Bellamy, who had a history of sexual offenses, but had never killed his victims. They looked toward Zarinsky because he had committed sexual offenses, coupled with murder.

Drug Store Beauty

In March of 1969, lovely seventeen-year-old Linda Balanabow was walking home from her job at a drug store in Linden. She had beautiful blonde hair and a delightful smile. Zarinsky pulled up in his white Ford Galaxy convertible and offered her a ride home. Although hesitant at first, this stocky man appeared to be no threat, so she climbed in.

Instead of driving her to her home in nearby Union, Zarinsky brought the girl to Woodbridge. She was screaming, but that didn't matter to him. He pulled over to the side of the road and climbed into the backseat. She tried to open the car door, but there were no door handles. He'd had them removed to prevent his victim's escape. She tried to kick him off, but to no avail. Although he was stocky, he was muscular.

He beat her mercilessly and blood spewed from her nose and mouth. Then he hit her on the head with a hammer. Zarinsky ripped off her blouse, bit her breasts and squeezed them until she hollered in pain. He pulled down her panties but didn't rape her.

Zarinsky came prepared with rope, a chain, a hammer, and an electrical cord. He used the rope to tie up her arms to keep them from pommeling him. Then he grabbed his chain and wrapped it around her neck and feet. That wasn't enough bondage to satisfy Zarinsky's warped sexual instincts, so he took out the electrical cord and tightened it around her tender neck. She writhed and struggled, desperately trying to catch a breath of oxygen. Then she gave up and died.

One of the greatest challenges facing killers is the disposal of the body. Zarinsky drove to Woodbridge in order to get to the Raritan River. He dragged her body from his car, wrapped her dress around her face then wedged rocks and pieces of concrete in her clothing to weigh the body down. With one move, he pitched her into the muddy river.

Balanabow's parents called the police. Sometimes teens run away from home and the police proposed that as a possibility. Linda's parents protested, saying she had no such tendencies and was a very happy girl.

On April 27 of that year, the parents were correct and the police were wrong. Linda's bloated body had floated to the surface and was identified by her grief-stricken parents. Her skull was cracked open and her jaw broken. It was a gruesome site.

Rosemary Calandriello

Seventeen-year-old Rosemary Calandriello took on a lot of responsibility for her family. They lived in the shore town of Atlantic Highlands. Ever since her father took ill, Rosemary did the shopping and took care of the family bills. She was an introverted girl and sheltered by her mother, but did have a few friends at high school.

On August 15, 1969, she went out to the store to pick up ice cream and milk. Her friends saw her get into a black Ford Galaxy with an older man. No one has seen her since. Her disappearance was reported to the police, who immediately suspected something because of Rosemary's uncharacteristic behavior.

The investigators met with the witnesses, and were able to get a composite sketch of the man in the car. Once the sketch was published in the newspapers, a local woman called the police, reporting that a mysterious man attempted to offer her twelve-year-old daughter and a friend a ride. The mother reported that the man reportedly promised them some wine, if they would climb into his car. They refused. As he pulled away, the girls wisely memorized the license plate number of the vehicle and gave it to police.

The authorities then tracked the plate to Zarinsky, and checked out his residence in Linden. When they drove up to his house, they noticed that he was washing out his car.

Immediately, they accosted him and he was arrested for corrupting the morals of two minors because he offered them alcohol. They also confiscated his car and brought it into the police garage for testing.

After examining the vehicle, investigators discovered that the inner door handles had been removed. In addition, they found a pair of hairclips, panties, and a ballpeen hammer with a chunk of flesh and a strand of human hair stuck to it. They then drove to the Calandriello home, and Rosemary's mother claimed the panties and clips belonged to her missing daughter.

Despite the mother's claim, Zarinsky's wife, Lynn, claimed the panties were hers but made no mention of the hair clips. That confused investigators, but the police continued to suspect Zarinsky, so their forensic team carefully analyzed the evidence. The hair they found in Zarinsky's car was also sent to the police lab for analysis.

In the meantime, Zarinsky was convicted of contributing to the delinquency of a minor and incarcerated. He filed for appeal, however, after which he was exonerated and released in 1972. After the police had combed through his car and collected evidence, they released his car.

University Co-Ed

Anne Logan, nineteen, was a freshman at Seton Hall University. She was excited about being accepted there since it was a nationally-recognized school. She lived in Garwood and commuted to college in her 1968 Cougar.

Anne worked at the Stop and Shop Supermarket on South Street, earning a few dollars in her part-time job. On April 18, 1973, Zarinsky was parked nearby and spotted Anne as she was getting into her car, which was parked around the corner on Eighth Street. It was quite late, so there were very few people around.

The urge to kill came over Zarinsky and his face flushed red. Suddenly, he became like a person possessed. In the madness of wild emotion, Zarinsky rushed at her. Anne knew some karate, and fought him off furiously, clawing at him with her fingernails. That surprised him, but made him even angrier. He snatched up a brick from the sidewalk and smashed her on the head with it. Blood gushed out, and soaked his T-shirt. Then he pulled down her pantyhose and raped her. To be sure she was dead, he choked her with the strap of her purse, after which he discarded his shirt and ran.

Anne Logan's body was found the next day by a passerby. She was lying in a pool of her own blood along with her disheveled clothes and Zarinsky's tell-tale T-shirt.

Doreen Carlucci and Joanne Delardo: Death at Christmas

On December 13, 1974, Doreen Carlucci, fourteen, and her friend, Joanne Delardo, fifteen, were dropped off by Delardo's father at the Parish Recreational Center where their church in Toms River was going to hold a Christmas dance. They walked down the street in their pretty dresses, very excited and looked forward to the affair.

The dance was fun, and they chatted as they walked toward the ice cream shop where they were going to be picked up. It was then ten in the evening. Joanne's father, John Delardo, was supposed to pick up the two girls, but he fell asleep on the couch. Mrs. Delardo woke up around midnight, with a start when she noticed Joanne wasn't home yet.

The Delardo's became alarmed, and called the Carlucci's. Mr. and Mrs. Carlucci hadn't suspected anything because they thought Doreen was going to spend the night with their daughter. All the parents were frantic. They called the police to report them missing and called on neighbors to help search for the pair. They posted pictures on telephone poles and the two girls' families offered a reward for their safe return.

Zarinsky celebrated the holiday by cruising around the streets of the shore towns he haunted. There, under the cover of night, his holiday fun came in the form of Joanne and Doreen. Zarinsky took sadistic pleasure in beating women. He savored seeing their pain. It gave him a sense of power, however perverted that was. But he didn't care.

Two long weeks later, a cyclist was riding along a sandy road about thirty miles away in Manalapan Township. Like Toms River, Manalapan was a shore town kissed by the salty air. On December 27, 1974, though, the chilled air of winter permeated the region, and that's when they found the girls—Doreen and Joanne lying lifeless on the edge of the path. Doreen was nearly nude and full of blackened bruises. She had been brutally strangled. Joanne was beaten and swollen and had an electrical cord wound tightly around her neck.

The Evidence Catches Up

In December of 1974, the prosecutor charged him with the murder of Rosemary Calandriello. Although her body was never found, they felt the authorities had a sufficient amount of evidence to bring him to trial.

Just a year later, in 1975, Zarinsky was convicted of the killing of Rosemary Calandriello. Zarinsky was then sentenced to life imprisonment.

During the process of analyzing Zarinsky's car, the forensic scientists identified the hair found on the ballpeen hammer in his back seat as belonging to Linda Balabano, who was killed in 1969.

Following that revelation, the police re-opened a number of unsolved cold cases of murders in the shore area. The authorities looked at the similar methods of the murders, and suspected him of the murders of Linda Balabano of Linden, Anne Logan of

Garwood, Jane Durrua of East Keansburg, Mary Klinsky of Hazlet, as well as Joanne Delardo and Doreen Carlucci of Toms River.

Confession

In 1988, while Robert Zarinsky was imprisoned in the South Woods State Prison in Bridgeton, New Jersey, he confessed to the murder of Rosemary Calandriello. He then quickly followed up his confession with the rationale that they had a fight, and afterwards, he accidentally rode over her with his car. Accidentally?

While in prison, Zarinsky bragged that he was responsible for about ten other murders. He didn't give specifics.

The Scramble for Zarinsky's Inheritance: Part One

Zarinsky's mother, Veronica, doted over him, even though he was a cruel youth who actually beat up his own father and sister, Judith.

In 1995, when Zarinsky's mother died, she willed him her mutual fund which contained one hundred twenty-one thousand dollars, some land, and their house in Linden. Judith received thirty thousand dollars in telecommunications stocks. The money was managed for him by Judith's daughter, Kimberly, and Zarinsky paid close attention to the funds each month.

Zarinsky's brother-in-law, Peter Sapsa became ill with congestive heart failure in 1997, and Judith went to her brother for a loan. He refused, thinking that he might be able to get paroled and would need the money then.

Judith and Peter were not only furious, but were in desperate need of the money for medical expenses. Judith was also ill, but afraid to return to Zarinsky again to beg for some money. They fell behind in their mortgage payments, their taxes, and couldn't afford a new car which they sorely needed. Judith had her husband, Peter, pose as Robert Zarinsky and drain the mutual fund of one hundred twelve thousand five hundred dollars.

When Zarinsky didn't get his monthly statement, he had the matter investigated. The postal inspector identified the photo of Peter Sapsa as the man who took the checks from the Zarinsky account. Zarinsky immediately knew what happened.

In 1999, Peter Sapsa was arrested for embezzlement, but Judy wasn't, even though she masterminded the plan. When Zarinsky heard of this, Judy wrote to him begging for forgiveness and offering him their house as retribution. Zarinsky showed no mercy.

161

Judith went to the police and accused her brother of killing Officer Charles Bernoski back in 1968, and how he and his accomplice had been shot in the process of the burglary at Miller Pontiac.

In 2000, Zarinsky was charged with the murder of the police officer. He categorically denied it, saying to CBS News, *"She did not see me come in shot by no police officer. She's making that up. She's lying to… for what she did to me, stealing everything."*

The Killing of Officer Bernoski Revisited

Once Zarinsky was charged with the murder of Officer Charles Bernoski, Elizabeth Bernoski, his widow, prepared a wrongful death suit against Zarinsky and Schiffer for the murder of her husband. In civil court, Elizabeth Bernoski won an award of nine point five million dollars. Of course, Zarinsky didn't have that money, so the courts settled on a payment of one hundred fifty-four thousand dollars, which was seized from Zarinsky's account.

The court indicated that Zarinsky had the right to retain some of the profits from his funds to finance his defense and subsequent appeals.

Judith Sapsa felt guilty about the conspiracy to embezzle Zarinsky's funds at that time, and was upset about implicating her husband in it. She consulted Detective Bill White of the Rahway Police Department near the murder scene when Officer Bernoski was shot and killed at Miller Pontiac back in 1958. As Judith discussed the case at length, White was astonished that she had such a keen memory for details.

She told him what happened when Zarinsky related the story about how he and his cousin, Ted Schiffer, robbed the dealership. Her narration raised questions in White's mind and he asked Frank Pfeiffer, the head investigator for the Union County Prosecutor's Office and State Trooper Coco to accompany him in an interview with Zarinsky's purported accomplice, Ted Schiffer.

This was forty years after the event, and Schiffer was now in a senior citizen's complex in Carbondale, Pennsylvania. He was sixty-one years old. White and Pfeiffer addressed Schiffer about the killing at the dealership, but he denied being there, indicating that Judith must be mistaken.

White then asked Schiffer to remove his shirt. Then he and Pfeiffer saw a scar on Schiffer's chest. When asked where he got the scar, he said, *"I fell on some barbed wire."*

It was clear to the men that the scar was the result of a gunshot wound. Schiffer was arrested and brought in for questioning. Trooper Coco took Schiffer's fingerprint and had it compared with the one found at Miller Pontiac. It was a match.

In 2001, a trial was held. Although many of the jurors believed that Zarinsky murdered Bernoski, there wasn't enough solid evidence to convict him. Thus, Zarinsky was acquitted of the murder of Charles Bernoski.

Because Schiffer's family lived in Pennsylvania, they asked that the court try him closer to their family home. The court agreed. Schiffer was then charged in Pennsylvania and given a fifteen year sentence. He died in 2007.

The Scramble for Zarinsky's Inheritance: Part Two

Because Zarinsky was acquitted of the murder of Bernoski, Zarinsky sued Bernoski's widow for the return of the money she had received in the wrongful death suit she won back in 2003. In 2004, Bernoski was allowed to keep it, but that decision was overturned and she was ordered to pay back the money with interest in 2007.

Because she'd given away most of the money to her children, the Police Benevolent Association (PBA) raised the funds. It was then put back into Zarinsky's account.

Trial for the Murder of Jane Durrua

In 2008, the prosecutor had enough evidence implicating him in the murder of Jane Durrua in 1968. On the day of his arraignment, Zarinsky was wheeled into the courtroom on a gurney. Zarinsky had a terminal case of pulmonary fibrosis, but the prosecutors were determined to let him know that justice demanded his presence. Zarinsky didn't care about his victims, and now the court didn't care about him.

The state had sufficient evidence against him in the Durrua case, as he was identified by Jane Durrua's friends upon looking at a sketch and a photo. They also had his license plate. In addition, they had proof that the murder was premeditated, making it a first-degree murder charge and a kidnapping as well. The kidnapping charge had to be dropped because the statute of limitations had expired. Too much time had intervened between the crime and the trial. The statute of limitations, though, never applies to murder.

Zarinsky died in prison in 2008, before that trial could be held.

Post-Mortem Penalty

The arm of the law is long. In 2009, Jane Conway and members of the family of Jane Durrua filed a wrongful death suit against the estate of Robert Zarinsky. Superior Court Judge Dennis O'Brien heard the case of Jane Durrua in civil court. It contended that Jane was "viciously attacked, assaulted, sexually assaulted, beaten, and battered." The attorneys in this case went after the funds that were frozen in escrow for the defense of Zarinsky.

When Zarinsky was first charged with this killing, DNA evidence hadn't been that well-developed. However, after the field of DNA analysis had greatly improved, the facts revealed in this case were instructive and absolutely indicated his guilt.

The Durrua family was awarded thirteen million dollars. They would never see all of that money, but were able to confiscate the one hundred twenty-six thousand dollars that Zarinsky had set aside for his defense.

Conclusion

NEW JERSEY LOOKS DELIGHTFUL ON A DAY IN early spring as the crocuses pop up their purple heads but it can be deceiving. It had its darkness hidden in the shadows of the dunes at the beach and the shadows of the city buildings in Newark. Its darkness was sometimes unseen, but it was a darkness traversed by many who have muddied it with the kind of evil only humans can create. The law-abiding population and the police have spent their lives washing its beautiful cities clean and creating a wonderland at the shore so that the Atlantic may wash up against it with salt water that renews it once again.

The New Jersey criminals of yesteryear are locked up or gone. New germs of evil are still growing, but those who know and love the state have been warned in advance to be more cautious than they would prefer to be.

This state, and indeed all other states, strive to make today better than yesterday. The garbage will be destroyed and the debris will be removed someday. The evil will eventually subside. Someday that will happen. But not today.

References

Blackwell, J. (2007) *Notorious New Jersey: 100 True Tales of Murders and Mobsters, Scandals and Scoundrels*. Rutgers University Press

Carlo, P. & Pritchard, M., et. al. (2007) *The Ice Man: Confessions of a Mafia Contract Killer*. St. Martin's Griffin

"Deputy Leader Grape Street Crips Gang" Retrieved from https://www.justice.gov/usao-nj/pr/deputy-leader-violent-grape-street-crips-gang-sentenced-45-years-prison-murder-attempted

"Eighteen Years for Duo who Ran Newark Drug Ring" Retrieved from https://www.justice.gov/usao-nj/pr/violent-gang-leader-sentenced-two-life-terms-ordering-six-murders-and-attempted-murder

Fisher, R. G., "Deadly Secrets," *The Star Ledger* Retrieved June 11, 2009

"Five Killings: A Fearful Silence is Broken" Retrieved from https://www.nytimes.com/1983/05/09/nyregion/five-killings-a-fearful-silence-is-broken.html

Good, M. E. "Rosemary K. Calandriello" *The Charley Project*. Retrieved February 27, 2016

King, J. (2008) *Murder and Mayhem in the Highlands: Historic Crimes of the Jersey Shore*. The History Press

"Long-time Leader: Violent Grape Street Crips Gang" Retrieved from https://www.justice.gov/usao-nj/pr/long-time-leader-violent-grape-street-crips-street-gang-and-two-members-convicted

O'Rourke, J. E. (2014) *The Jersey Shore Thrill Killer: Richard Biegenwald*. Kindle Publishing

"U.S. Court vs Corey Hamlet" Retrieved from https://www.justice.gov/usao-nj/press-release/file/1080376/download "U.S. District Court vs Corey Hamlet et. al."

"Violent Gang Leader Sentenced to Two Life Terms" Retrieved from https://www.justice.gov/usao-nj/pr/violent-gang-leader-sentenced-two-life-terms-ordering-six-murders-and-attempted-murder

Acknowledgements

This is a special thanks to the following readers who have taken time out of their busy schedule to be part of the True Crime Seven Team. Thank you all so much for all the feedback and support!

James, Rebecca Donnell, Jo Donna Hoevet, Joan Baker, Jamie Bothen, Dezirae, Christy Riemenschneider, Donna Reif, Marcie Walters, Kathy Morgan, Anna Mccown, Jason C. Tillery, Tina Shattuck, Lee Fowley, Sandy Van Domelen, Rebecca Ednie, Paul Kelley, Jo-Lee Sears, Lee Barta, Beth Alfred, Cindy Harcar, Judy Stephens, Susan M. Leedy, Jami Bridgman, Huw, Angie Grafton, Rachel B, Dannnii Desjarlais, Jeanie, Amanda, Irene Dobson, Annette Estrella, Remy Tankel-Carroll, Sherry Whitaker, Patricia Jeter, Tim Haight, Joy Page, Latrena Shultz, Donna, Natalie Gwinn, Tara Pendley, Libertysusan Gabor, Amanda Gallegos, John, Gordon Carmichael, James, Bessie, Damon Geddins, Toni Marie Rinella, Merja Mikkonen, Landa-Lou Goodridge, Wanda Jones, Barbara English, Shane Neely, Allyssa Howells, Jason Barnum, Kurt Brown, Connie White, Muhammad Nizam Bin Mohtar, Cindy Sirois, Teresa, Jason, Amanda, Jannis M. Fetter, Julie Descant, Christopher, Karin Dennis, Lynne Ridley, Sena Schneider, Melissa Swain, Jennifer Hanlon, Shanon Taylor, Dani Bigner, Rita, Jennifer Lloyd, Kelly, Amy Steagall Johnson, Monde Magolo, Anj Panes, Sandra Driskell, Marshall Bellitire, Amanda Kliebert, Ole Pedersen, Joyce Carroll, Kristin Schroeder, Michelle Babb, Kim Thurston, Shakila "Kiki" Robinson, Laurel Von Dobschutz, Sue Wells, Larry J. Field, Linda Blackburn, Cory Lindsey, Deborah Sparagna, Michelle Lee, Cathy Russell, Adele Buckle, Sue Wallace, Tammy Sittlinger, Chris Hurte, Felix Sacco, Mark Sawyer, Andrew Ayers, Deborah Hanson, Alan Kleynenberg, Tamela L. Matuska, Sherry Sundin, Chad Mellor, Susan Weaver, Monica Yokel, Linda Shoemaker, Tina Rattray-Green, Susan Ault, Samantha Watt, Shelia Clark, Michele Gosselin, Karen Smith, Alicia Gir, Casey Renee Bates, Shannon Fiene, Cara Butcher, Rebecca Roberts, Jennifer Jones, Lolly Caviness, Adrian Brown, Marcia Heacock, Lisa Slat, Amy Hart, Richard Allen, Deirdre Green, Paula Lookabill, Bambi Dawn Goggio, Diane Kourajian, Abriel Miller, Jon Wiederhorn, Linda J Evans, Diane Kremski, Tina Bullard, Crystal Clark, Jamie Rasmussen, Myene Kelley, Melody

Sanderson, Awilda Roman, Don Price, Patricia Fulton, Eoin Corr, Cindy Selby, Amy Edwards, Debbie Hill, Robyn Byers, Nancy Harrison, Leigh Morrow, Miranda Sowers, Matthew Lawson, Bill Willoughby, Joy Riester, Alex Slocomb, David Edmonds, Bob Carter, Jennifer Sawyer, Tammy Hart, Robert Upton, Alexander Belyatsky, Kristi Horn, Joey Marie Coulombe, Laura Rouston, Warwick Dowler, Robert Fritsch, Marion E. M. Newman, Michelle Laing

Continue Your Exploration Into

The Murderous Mind

Excerpt From True Crime Explicit

Volume 1

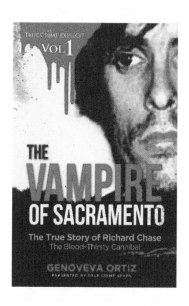

Introduction

HUMANS ARE FASCINATED BY EVIL. POP culture is full of mad men, killers, and monsters who have become iconic characters, and sometimes are even more beloved than the heroes.

Villains make a story interesting, and no matter how depraved they may be, there is always a part of us that almost wants to see them win. After all, the higher the stakes, the more powerful the story.

When we get older, however, we learn that true evil really does exist. A real-life villain does not need to be a criminal mastermind or a mad scientist. Sometimes, evil is merely a human being hiding in plain sight.

Human monsters can turn our world upside down. Suddenly, the neighborhoods we have called home all our lives become dangerous, and the people we call our friends become suspects. When a killer strikes, can the people around the victims ever feel safe again?

Richard Chase changed the lives of multiple people in the most nightmarish ways imaginable. It was not enough for him to simply take the lives of his victims; he also drank their blood and violated their bodies for his own twisted curiosity. He killed without remorse, and scariest of all, he killed without rhyme or reason. Anyone was fair game to the *Vampire of Sacramento*.

But at the end of the day, Richard Chase was still only human, and his story is not only one of horror and disgust, but also a tragedy about an extremely sick person who was failed by his family and mental health professionals alike. Had someone taken Chase's alarming behavior seriously when he was young, would six innocent people still be alive?

Was Chase destined to become a killer, or did life mold him into one?

This book will explore not only the terrible crimes perpetrated by one of the world's most horrific and depraved murderers, but also examine the social conditions that allowed him to become a monster.

 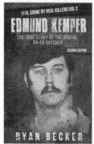  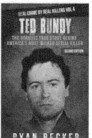

About True Crime Seven

True Crime Seven Books is about exploring the stories behind all the murderous minds in the world. From unknown murderers to infamous serial killers.

Our writers come from all walks of life but with one thing in common, and that is they are all true crime enthusiasts. You can learn more about them below:

Ryan Becker is a True Crime author who started his writing journey in late 2016. Like most of you, he loves to explore the process of how individuals turn their darkest fantasies into a reality. Ryan has always had a passion for storytelling. So, writing is the best output for him to combine his fascination with psychology and true crime. It is Ryan's goal for his readers to experience the full immersion with the dark reality of the world, just like how he used to in his younger days.

Nancy Alyssa Veysey is a writer and author of true crime books, including the bestselling, *Mary Flora Bell: The Horrific True Story Behind an Innocent Girl Serial Killer.* Her medical degree and work in the field of forensic psychology, along with postgraduate studies in criminal justice, criminology, and pre-law, allow her to bring a unique perspective to her writing.

Kurtis-Giles Veysey is a young writer who began his writing career in the fantasy genre. In late 2018, he parlayed his love and knowledge of history into writing nonfiction accounts of true crime stories that occurred in centuries past. Told from a historical perspective, Kurtis-Giles brings these victims and their killers back to life with vivid descriptions of these heinous crimes.

Kelly Gaines is a writer from Philadelphia. Her passion for storytelling began in childhood and carried into her college career. She received a B.A. in English from Saint Joseph's University in 2016, with a concentration in Writing Studies. Now part of the real world, Kelly enjoys comic books, history documentaries, and a good scary story. In her true-crime work, Kelly focuses on the motivations of the killers and backgrounds of the victims to draw a complete picture of each individual. She deeply enjoys writing for True Crime Seven and looks forward to bringing more spine-tingling tales to readers.

James Parker, the pen-name of a young writer from New Jersey, who started his writing journey with play-writing. He has always been fascinated with the psychology of murderers and how the media might play a role in their creation. James loves to constantly test out new styles and ideas in his writing so one day he can find something cool and unique to himself.

Brenda Brown is a writer and an illustrator-cartoonist. Her art can be found in books distributed both nationally and internationally. She has also written many books related to her graduate degree in psychology and her minor in history. Like many true crime enthusiasts, she loves exploring the minds of those who see the world as a playground for expressing the darker side of themselves—the side that people usually locked up and hid from scrutiny.

Genoveva Ortiz is a Los Angeles-based writer who began her career writing scary stories while still in college. After receiving a B.A. in English in 2018, she shifted her focus to nonfiction and the real-life horrors of crime and unsolved mysteries. Together with True Crime Seven, she is excited to further explore the world of true crime through a social justice perspective.

You can learn more about us and our writers at:

truecrimeseven.com/about

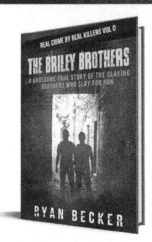

Dark Fantasies Turned Reality

Prepare yourself, we're not going to **hold back on details or cut out any of the gruesome truths...**